Army Badges and Insignia of World War 2

U.S., Great Britain, Poland, Belgium, Italy, U.S.S.R., Germany

Army Badges and Insignia of World War 2

U.S., Great Britain, Poland, Belgium,
Italy, U.S.S.R., Germany

by

Guido Rosignoli

THE MACMILLAN COMPANY
NEW YORK, NEW YORK

THE MACMILLAN COMPANY
866 Third Avenue, New York, NY 10022

Library of Congress Catalog Card No. 72-85765

First American Edition 1972

Printed in Great Britain

Contents

Introduction

During the last decade I have noticed an increasing interest in military matters; an interest that is growing all over the world. I have also found that in every country the collector concentrates upon the militaria of his own national armed forces and upon that of one foreign army whose exploits have particularly fascinated the popular imagination. The latter, in most cases, is the Nazi German Army.

As, unfortunately, very little contact exists among collectors of different nationalities, there is limited common knowledge about each other's collections. This lack of knowledge often prevents the collector from extending his interest to the many unfamiliar bargains displayed on the stalls of our local markets.

In this book I hope to widen the scope of the collector, and have illustrated and described the badges worn during World War 2 by the armies of seven countries who were major combatants. The order in which they appear has been solely established by the availability of information and partly by printing necessities.

I have supplemented the illustrations with brief historical backgrounds and descriptions of the uniforms on which the badges were worn, although I do not mention the uniforms of special regiments and traditional garments, as they are beyond the scope of this particular volume.

Additional lists of coloured cap bands and trouser stripes have been provided, together with lists of regimental and divisional titles and any other information that could be of use to the military historian.

I regret that space limitations have compelled me to deal solely with the regular armies and, in the case of the Polish and Belgian Armies, to illustrate only the badges of the 1939–40 period.

Uniforms and badges have always been controlled by the official army dress regulations and as the majority of participants entered World War 2 with uniforms and equipment adopted in the early 1930s, I have found it necessary in some cases to show badges in use long before that war.

Although most modern armies nowadays are apparently similar, they differ in their structural organisation, owing to different historical backgrounds and different traditions. Some armies have branches of service, or even rank titles, that have no counterpart in the armies of other nations. For instance, some books published in Britain and the U.S.A. have translated German N.C.O.s rank titles into British and American N.C.O.s

7

rank titles respectively.   I have chosen to translate the ranks literally for what they are.   American terms have been used in the section dedicated to the U.S. Army, so that the term 'shoulder patch' replaces the British 'formation sign', although the American term 'enlisted men' has been generally replaced with the term 'other ranks'.

Where it has been impossible to translate accurately I have employed the foreign term.

G. Rosignoli,
Farnham, Surrey, 1972

Author's Note

I would like to thank the following for the assistance they gave me while I was compiling this book:

The Belgian Embassy
The Embassy of the U.S.S.R
The Embassy of the U.S.A.
Mr. Henry Brown, M.B.E., General Secretary of the Commando Association
Captain W. Milewski, the Curator, and Captain R. Dembinski of the Polish Institute and Sikorski Museum
Mr. K. Barbarsk for his untiring help
Mr. L Granata of Trieste
Mr. L. Milner of the Imperial War Museum for his help with the German section
Mr. E. C. M. Williams for his help with translations

I would also like to acknowledge both the assistance I have had, and the pleasure I have personally gained, from the many magnificently equipped regimental museums I have visited both here and in Europe.

The Illustrations

The badges illustrated on the following plates are drawn only in approximate proportion to each other. The reader will appreciate that an exact proportion could not have been worked out satisfactorily because of the great variations in sizes of these badges.

As far as the colours of the branches of service are concerned, it should be taken into consideration when reading the text that I have used the colour description of the country concerned.

For instance, although the 'colours' of the Medical Services of Britain, the U.S.A., Belgium, Italy and Poland are a similar shade of red, each country has adopted its own definition of the colour, and so the Medical Service of the U.S.A. has maroon, Great Britain dull cherry, Belgium and Italy amaranth and Poland cherry red.

The Illustrations

CAP BADGES AND GORGET PATCHES

Generals   Field-marshal   General   Brigadier   Brigadier

OFFICER'S RANK BADGES

Field-marshal   General   Lieutenant-general   Major-general

Brigadier   Colonel   Lieutenant-colonel   Major

Captain   Lieutenant   2nd lieutenant

PLATE 1

WARRANT OFFICERS' RANK BADGES

4   5

1. Regimental sergeant-major of the Foot Guards   2. Staff sergeant-major (1st Class) and conductors   3. Regimental corporal-major and Farriers corporal-major of the Household Cavalry and W.O. (1st Class)   4. Regimental quartermaster-corporal and Farriers quarter-master-corporal of the Household Cavalry and quartermaster-sergeant of the Foot Guards   5. Squadron corporal-major of the Royal Horse Guard and W.O. (2nd Class)

NON-COMMISSIONED OFFICERS' RANK BADGES

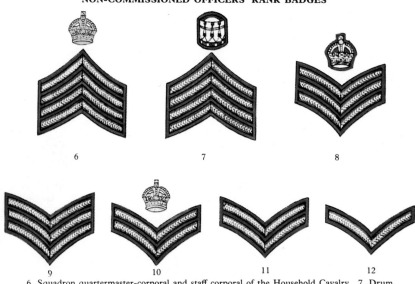

6   7   8

9   10   11   12

6. Squadron quartermaster-corporal and staff corporal of the Household Cavalry   7. Drum major   8. Corporal-of-horse of the Household Cavalry, quartermaster-sergeant, colour-sergeant and staff-sergeant   9. Sergeant   10. Corporal and lance-corporal of the Household Cavalry   11. Corporal, bombardier (R.A.)   12. Lance-corporal and lance-bombardier (R.A.).

PLATE 2

FORMATION SIGNS

Supreme Headquarters, British and Allied Forces

G.H.Q. Home Forces G.H.Q. India Allied Forces H.Q. A.L.F.S.E.A. S.A.C.S.E.A.

S.H.A.E.F. 15th Army Group 21st Army Group C.M.F.

Armies

1st 2nd 8th 9th 10th 12th 14th

Army Corps

1st 2nd 3rd 4th 5th 8th 9th(1st)

10th 11th 12th 13th 25th 30th 9th(2nd)

PLATE 3

GREAT BRITAIN

FORMATION SIGNS
Armoured Divisions

Guards   1st   2nd   6th   7th(1st)   7th(2nd)

8th   9th   10th   11th   42nd   79th

Armoured Brigades

4th   6th   7th   8th   9th   16th

20th   22nd   23rd   25th   27th   31st

33rd   34th   35th   1st Armd Repl. Group C.M.F.

Army Tank Brigades

21st(1st)   21st(2nd)   23rd   24th   25th   36th

PLATE 4

CAP BADGES
Cavalry and Armoured Regiments

L.G.

R.H.G.

K.D.G.

Bays

3 D.G.

4/7 D.G.

5 Innis D.G.

Royals

Greys

3 H.

'4 H.

7 H.

8 H.

9 L.

10 H.

11 H.

PLATE 5

GREAT BRITAIN

12 L.

13/18 H.

14/20 H.

15/19 H.

16/5 L.

17/21 L.

22 D.

23 H.

24 L.

25 D.

26 H.

27 L.

R.T.R.

R.A.C.

Recce

PLATE 6

CAP BADGES

Corps, Administrative Departments, etc.

R.A.

R.H.A.

H.A.C.
(Infantry)

H.A.C.

R.E.

R.A.S.C.

R.Sigs

R.A.O.C.

R.A.M.C.

M.P.

M.P.S.C.

R.A.V.C.

A.A.C.

A.D.C.

R.E.M.E.

I.C.

PLATE 7

GREAT BRITAIN

CAP BADGES
Corps, Administrative Departments, etc.

R.A.P.C.

A.P.T.C.

R.P.C.

A.E.C.

G.S.C.

A.C.C.

G.S.C.

P.R.

G.G.

Foot Guards

W.G.

C.G.

S.G.

I.G.

PLATE 8

CAP BADGES

Infantry of the Line

R.S.

Queen's

Buffs.

King's Own

N.F.

Warwick

R.F.

King's

Norfolk

Lincolns

Devon

Suffolk

Som.L.I.

W.Yorks

E.Yorks.

Bedfs. Herts.

PLATE 9

CAP BADGES

Infantry of the Line

Leicesters

Green Howards

L.F.

R.S.F.

Cheshire

R.W.F.

S.W.B.

K.O.S.B.

Cameronians

Innisks.

Glosters.

Worc.R.

E.Lan.R.

Surreys

D.C.L.I.

D.W.R.

PLATE 10

CAP BADGES

Infantry of the Line

Border

R. Sussex

Hamps.

S.Staffords

Dorset

S.Lan.R.

Welch

Black Watch

Oxf.Bucks.

Essex

Foresters

Loyals

Northamptons

R.Berks.

R.W.K.

K.O.Y.L.I.

K.S.L.I.

PLATE 11

CAP BADGES
Infantry of the Line

Mx.

K.R.R.C.

Wilts.

Manch.

N.Staffs.

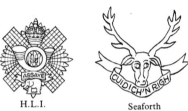

Y. & L.

D.L.I.

H.L.I.

Seaforth

Gordons

R.U.R.

R.Ir.F.

A. & S.H.

R.B.

L.R.

H.R.

PLATE 12

FORMATION SIGNS
Infantry Divisions

1st

2nd

3rd

4th

5th

6th

9th

12th

13th

15th

18th

23rd

36th

38th

40th

43rd

44th

45th

46th

47th

48th

49th

50th

51st

52nd

53rd

54th

55th

56th

59th

61st

76th

77th

78th

80th

PLATE 13

GREAT BRITAIN

FORMATION SIGNS

Independent Infantry Brigades and Brigade Groups

1st

24th

29th

31st

32nd

33rd

36th

37th

38th

56th

61st

70th

71st

72nd

73rd

115th

116th

148th

204th

206th

212th

214th

218th

219th

223rd

227th

231st

301st

303rd

304tn

Recce, 4th Division

133rd

H.Q. Pack Transp. Group, C.M.F.

PLATE 14

AIRBORNE FORCES

SPECIAL FORCES CAP BADGES

No 2 Commando   R.S.R.   S.A.S.   L.R.D.G.   'V' Force

No 6 Commando   Nos 50-52 Commandos

P.P.A.

WINGS

1st Glider Pilots   2nd Glider Pilots   S.A.S.

Parachutists

PLATE 15

COMMANDO SHOULDER FLASHES

No 1 Commando

Combined Operations

Commando Signals

Commandos

3 COMMANDO

4 COMMANDO

Nº 6 COMMANDO

101 Troop

5 COMMANDO

V COMMANDO

'V' Force

COMMANDO SBS

Special Boat Service

H.Q. Special Service Bde

SPECIAL IV SERVICE

COMMANDO D

Depot

5 Troop

TWELVE

TWELVE COMMANDO

FIRST COMMANDO BRIGADE

VI COMMANDO

PLATE 16

OFFICERS' RANK BADGES
worn on peaked cap

Generals

Senior officers

Junior officers

collar patches

Generals

Officers

worn on the shoulder straps

Marshal

General of Army

General of Division

General of Brigade

PLATE 17

POLAND

OFFICERS' RANK BADGES
worn on the shoulder straps

Marshal

Colonel

Lieutenant-colonel

General

Major

Captain

Lieutenant

2nd Lieutenant

MONOGRAMS FOR CAVALRY SHOULDER STRAPS

1 L.H.   3 L.H.   2 L.   7 L.   8 L.   11 L.   16 L.   17 L.   19 L.

20 L.   26 L.   27 L.   3 M.R.   6 M.R.   9 M.R.

PLATE 18

WARRANT OFFICERS AND N.C.Os' RANK BADGES
on coloured cap bands

| W.O. | Staff-sergeant | Sergeant | Lance-sergeant | Corporal | Lance-corporal |

collar patches

Warrant officers and sergeants   Other ranks

shoulder straps

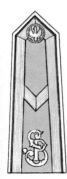    

W.O.   Staff-sergeant   Sergeant

Cadet
(Reg.Army)

Cadet
(Reserve)

Lance-sergeant   Corporal   Lance-corporal

PLATE 19

POLAND

COLLAR PATCHES

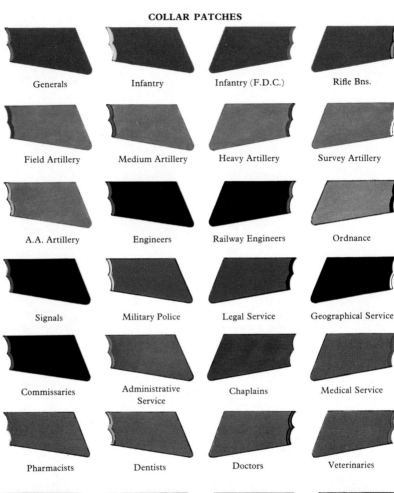

Generals

Infantry

Infantry (F.D.C.)

Rifle Bns.

Field Artillery

Medium Artillery

Heavy Artillery

Survey Artillery

A.A. Artillery

Engineers

Railway Engineers

Ordnance

Signals

Military Police

Legal Service

Geographical Service

Commissaries

Administrative Service

Chaplains

Medical Service

Pharmacists

Dentists

Doctors

Veterinaries

Cavalry

Horse Artillery

Mounted Pioneers

Cav. Squadrons (F.D.C.)

Recce (Mot.Bde)

Anti-Tank (Mot.Bde)

Signal Sq.

Train

Armoured units

PLATE 20

COLLAR PATCHES
Light Horse

1st Regt.   2nd Regt.   3rd Regt.

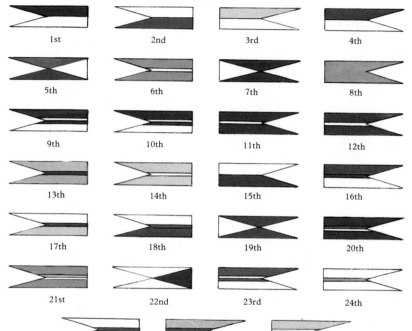

Lancers

1st   2nd   3rd   4th

5th   6th   7th   8th

9th   10th   11th   12th

13th   14th   15th   16th

17th   18th   19th   20th

21st   22nd   23rd   24th

25th   26th   27th

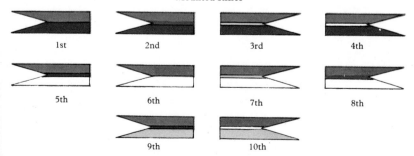

Mounted Rifles

1st   2nd   3rd   4th

5th   6th   7th   8th

9th   10th

PLATE 21

POLAND

COLLAR BADGES

General Staff

Geographical Service

Commissaries

Naval Service

11th Mtd. Division

21st/22nd Mtd. Division

Chaplains

Craftsmen

N.C.O. Schools

Bandmaster

Bandsman

1st (Tartar) Sq.
13 L.

37th Inf. Regt.

40th

44th

58th

H.Q. 16th Inf.Div.

63rd

64th

65th

66th

74th

82nd

84th

85th

PLATE 22

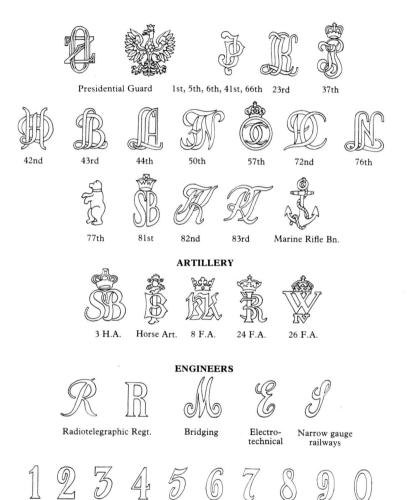

POLAND

MONOGRAMS AND BADGES FOR INFANTRY SHOULDER STRAPS

Presidential Guard   1st, 5th, 6th, 41st, 66th   23rd   37th

42nd   43rd   44th   50th   57th   72nd   76th

77th   81st   82nd   83rd   Marine Rifle Bn.

ARTILLERY

3 H.A.   Horse Art.   8 F.A.   24 F.A.   26 F.A.

ENGINEERS

Radiotelegraphic Regt.   Bridging   Electro-technical   Narrow gauge railways

PLATE 23

POLAND

INFANTRY REGIMENTAL BADGES

Officers School
(Reg. Army)

Officers School
(Reserve)

Officers School
for N.C.O.

Training Centre

1st Regt.

2nd

3rd

4th

5th

6th

7th

8th

9th

10th

11th

12th

13th

14th

15th

16th

17th

18th

19th

20th

21st

22nd

23rd

24th

25th

PLATE 24

INFANTRY REGIMENTAL BADGES

26th 27th 28th 29th 30th

31st 32nd 33rd 34th 35th

36th 37th 38th 39th 40th

41st 42nd 43rd 44th 45th

48th 49th 50th 51st 52nd

53rd 54th 55th 56th 57th

PLATE 25

POLAND

INFANTRY REGIMENTAL BADGES

58th   59th   60th   61st   62nd

63rd   64th   65th   66th   67th

68th   69th   70th   71st   72nd

73rd   74th   75th   76th   77th

78th   79th   80th   81st   82nd

83rd   84th   85th   86th

PLATE 26

HIGHLAND RIFLE REGIMENTS AND RIFLE BATTALIONS

1st. H.R. Regt	2nd	3rd	4th	5th
6th	1st. Rifle Bn.	2nd	3rd	Marine Rifle Bn.

CAVALRY

School	1st Light Horse Regt.	2nd	3rd
1st Lancers	2nd	3rd	4th	5th
6th	7th	8th	9th	10th

PLATE 27

POLAND

CAVALRY

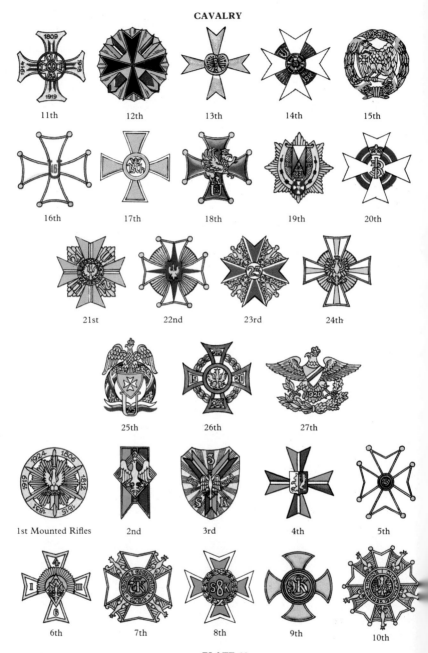

11th   12th   13th   14th   15th

16th   17th   18th   19th   20th

21st   22nd   23rd   24th

25th   26th   27th

1st Mounted Rifles   2nd   3rd   4th   5th

6th   7th   8th   9th   10th

PLATE 28

FIELD ARTILLERY

1st F.A. Regt.   2nd   3rd   4th   5th

6th   7th   8th   9th   10th

11th   12th   13th   14th   15th

16th   17th   18th   19th   20th

21st   22nd   23rd   24th   25th

26th   27th   28th   29th   30th

PLATE 29

POLAND

ARTILLERY

1st Medium Art. Regt.

2nd

3rd

4th

5th

6th

7th

8th

9th

10th

1st Heavy Art. Regt.

Horse Art.

Art. Officers Sch.

Survey Art.

1st Motorised Art. Regt.

31st F.A. Regt.

1st A.A. Art. Regt.

A.A. Artillery

Cadet Force Instr.

PROFICIENCY BADGES

Sword-Lance

Rifle Association

National Sport badge

Riding

Marksman

PLATE 30

ENGINEERS AND SIGNALS

Eng. School

Fortifications

Training
Centre

Officers' School
Regular Army Reserve

1st Bn.

2nd

3rd

4th

7th

8th

9th—6th

1st Railway Bn.

Mounted
Pioneers

Bridging Bn.

Signals
Corps

Signals
School

Signals Officers'
School

Signals Tr.
Centre

Radio Tr.
Signals

1st Telegraphic Bn.

5th

7th

1st Signals Regt.

Electro-Techn. Bn.

PLATE 31

POLAND

ARMOURED TROOPS

Armd. Corps   A.C. Training Centre   1st Armd. Bn.   2nd   3rd

4th   5th   6th   7th   8th

9th   10th   12th   1st Armd. Train. Group   2nd

SERVICES, SCHOOLS, ETC.

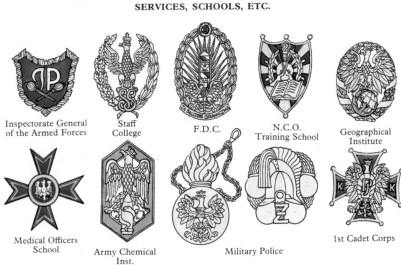

Inspectorate General of the Armed Forces   Staff College   F.D.C.   N.C.O. Training School   Geographical Institute

Medical Officers School   Army Chemical Inst.   Military Police   1st Cadet Corps

PLATE 32

NATIONAL COCKADE

CAP BANDS

Generals   Colonel-brigadier

COLLAR PATCHES AND SHOULDER STRAPS

Colonel-brigadier (Infantry)

Lieutenant-general   Major-general

General's badge for
shoulder cords

PLATE 33

Officers' belt buckle

BELGIUM

RANK BADGES

Officers

Senior officers
Chass. of the Ardennes

Junior officers
Grenadiers

Corps and Services

Colonel
Gen. Staff (Inf.)

Colonel
Chasseurs-on-Foot

Lieutenant-colonel
Engineers-Signals

Major
Grenadiers

Captain-commandant
Chasseurs-on-Horse

Captain
Artillery

Lieutenant
Carabiniers

2nd Lieutenant
Transport Corps

Warrant Officers

W.O. 1st Class
Frontier Cyclists Regt.

Lancers

W.O.
Carab. Cyclists

PLATE 34

RANK BADGES

Sergeants and Corporals

Sergeants
Administrative Service

Corporals and privates
Transport Corps

Chevrons

Sergeant-major   1st Sergeant   Sergeant   Corporal   Private 1st Class

Corps and Services

Guides

Chass. of the
Ardennes

Commissaries

Light Horse

Lancers

Doctors

Pharmacists

Dentists

Veterinaries

Medical Service
(O.R.)

Legal Service

Administrative Service

Military Supplies

PLATE 35

BELGIUM

OFFICERS' BADGES ON PEAKED CAP, JACKET AND GREATCOAT

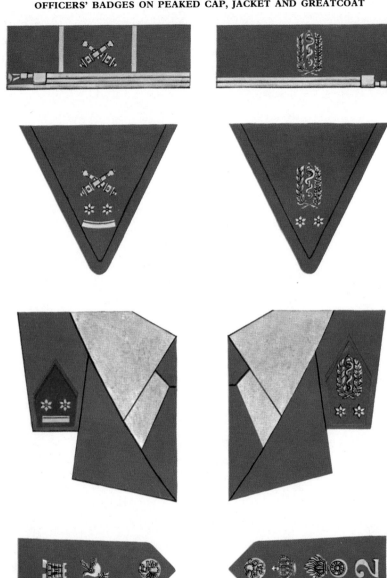

Lieutenant-colonel (Artillery)

Lieutenant (doctor—Medical Service)

PLATE 36

CORPS AND SERVICE BADGES

Carabiniers

Chasseurs-
on-Foot

Grenadiers

Chasseurs of
the Ardennes

Fortress
units

Cavalry

Chasseurs-
on-Horse

Cyclists

Light Horse

Guides

Lancers

Artillery   Horse Artillery

Cav. Depot

Art. Depot

Infantry

Mot. Artillery

A.A. Artillery

Fortress
Namur

Regiments
Liege

Artillery Repair
Service

Military
Railways

Pontoon Service

Signals

Transports H.Q.

Transport Corps

River Transport

Camouflage Service

Commissariat
(other ranks)

Road-River ways
Maintenance

Engineers

Band

Water Suppliers

PLATE 37

BELGIUM

CORPS AND SERVICE BADGES

Chaplains

Catholic, Protestant and Jewish Chaplains

Civilian Personnel

Medical, Veterinary
and Pharmacist Services
(other ranks)

REGIMENTAL, ARMY CORPS NUMERALS

1234567890

'ATTRIBUTES DES FONCTIONS'

Generals

General Staff

Commissaries

Medical, Veterinary
and Pharmacist officers

Administrative
officers

Officers-N.C.O.
archivist secretaries

Officers
Military Supplies

N.C.O. secretaries
of Commissariat

Officers-N.C.O.
quartermasters

Aerostat
officers

Advocate generals

Judge advocates

Clerks

PLATE 38

ITALY

GENERALS' RANK BADGES
worn on peaked cap

First Marshal of the Empire

Marshal of Italy and Generals

on field service cap
1934-35

1935-43

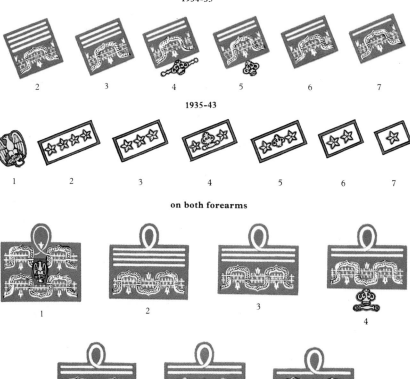

on both forearms

1. First Marshal of the Empire   2. Marshal of Italy   3. General of Army   4. General "in command" of an Army   5. General of Army Corps   6. General of Division   7. General of Brigade.

PLATE 39

ITALY

OFFICERS' RANK BADGES
worn on peaked cap

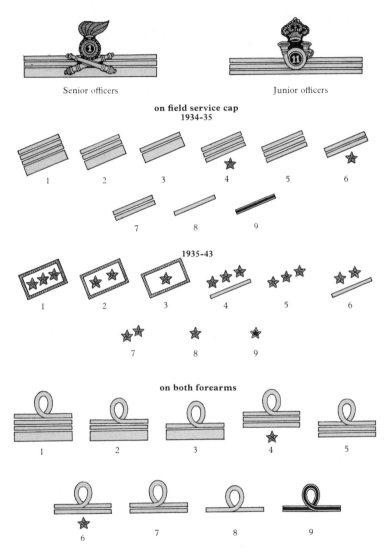

Senior officers

Junior officers

on field service cap
1934–35

1935–43

on both forearms

1. Colonel   2. Lieutenant-colonel   3. Major   4. First captain   5. Captain   6. 1st Lieutenant
7. Lieutenant   8. 2nd Lieutenant   9. Cadet

PLATE 40

WARRANT OFFICERS' RANK BADGES

worn on peaked cap

worn on shoulder straps

Aiutante di battaglia W.O. Major Chief W.O. W.O.

NON-COMMISSIONED OFFICERS AND OTHER RANKS
worn on both forearms (1909-1939)

Sergeant-major Sergeant Corporal-major Corporal

on both upper arms (since 1939)

Sergeant-major Sergeant Corporal-major Corporal

PLATE 41

ITALY

COLLAR PATCHES

Infantry   Grenadiers   Cavalry

Commiss.   Unass. Inf.   Art.   Eng.   Admin.   Med.

Vet.   Fencing Instr.   Supply   G.A.F.

M.G.   Mortars   Mot. M.G.

Div. Scout Group   Divisional Art.   Div. Eng.   Mot. Inf.

Tanks   Light Tanks   Motor Transport

Mot. Artillery   Alpine Art.

Bersaglieri   10th Assault Regt.   *Alpini*   Alpine Eng.

Guastatori   Chemical Centre   Parachutists   Para-*Guast.*

General Staff   M.V.S.N.   'M' Bns.   Adjutant

PLATE 42

CAP BADGES

Infantry	*Bersaglieri*	Colonial Rifles	Mot. Infantry
Parachutists	Grenadiers	Tanks	Light Tanks
Dragoons	Lancers	Cavalry	Cav. Depot
10th Assault Regt.	Motor Transport		Chemical Centre

PLATE 43

ITALY

CAP BADGES

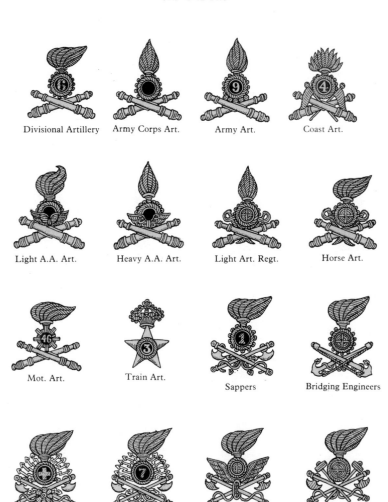

Divisional Artillery   Army Corps Art.   Army Art.   Coast Art.

Light A.A. Art.   Heavy A.A. Art.   Light Art. Regt.   Horse Art.

Mot. Art.   Train Art.   Sappers   Bridging Engineers

Signals (Radio)   Signals   Railway Engineers   Miners

PLATE 44

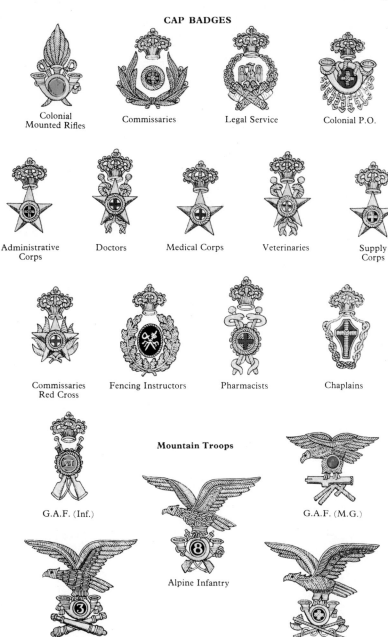

CAP BADGES

Colonial
Mounted Rifles

Commissaries

Legal Service

Colonial P.O.

Administrative
Corps

Doctors

Medical Corps

Veterinaries

Supply
Corps

Commissaries
Red Cross

Fencing Instructors

Pharmacists

Chaplains

G.A.F. (Inf.)

Mountain Troops

G.A.F. (M.G.)

Alpine Infantry

Alpine Artillery

Alpine Engineers

PLATE 45

ITALY

DIVISIONAL ARM SHIELDS

Infantry Divisions   Motorised Divisions   Alpine Division

ARM AND BREAST BADGES

G.A.F.

Assault

Guastatori

1   2

Parachutists

3   4

CAP BADGES

Alpini   Medical Corps

Bersaglieri

OTHER BADGES

Gilded pioneer badge

Silvered Infantry badge

Brass shoulder plate
(Sergeants, corporals & privates)

Grenadiers' plate worn
on ammunition pouch

PLATE 46

EARLY FASCIST CAP BADGES

Officers   Generals   Black Shirts

MILIZIA VOLONTARIA SICUREZZA NAZIONALE
1923-38

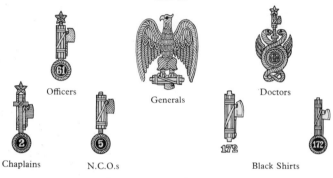

Officers   Generals   Doctors

Chaplains   N.C.O.s   Black Shirts

1938-43

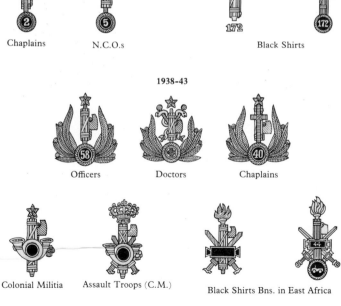

Officers   Doctors   Chaplains

Colonial Militia   Assault Troops (C.M.)   Black Shirts Bns. in East Africa

PLATE 47

ITALY

M.V.S.N. RANK BADGES

worn on both forearms
1923–35

1   2   3   4

5   6   7   8

1923–31

9   10   11

worn on headgear
1923–35

1   2   3   3   4

1923–30   1923–43

5   6   7   8

1923–43

9   10   11

1. Comandante generale 2. Luogotenente generale 3. Console generale 4. Console
5. Primo seniore 6. Seniore 7. Centurione 8. Capo manipolo 9. Capo squadra 10. Vice
capo squadra 11. Camicia Nera scelta

PLATE 48

worn on both forearms
1935-38

1 3 4 5

1938-43

1 2 3 4 5

1935-43

6 7 8 9 10

11

1931-38

15 16 17 18

shoulder straps

on both upper arms
1938-43

15 16

17 18

12 13 14

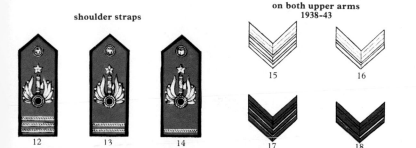

1. Comandante generale 2. Luogotenente generale (Chief of Staff) 3. Luogotenente generale
4. Console generale 5. Console 6. Primo seniore 7. Seniore 8. Centurione 9. Capo
manipolo 10. Sottocapo manipolo 11. Aspirante 12. Primo aiutante 13. Aiutante capo
14. Aiutante 15. Primo capo squadra 16. Capo squadra 17. Vice capo squadra 18. Camicia
Nera scelta

PLATE 49

ITALY

M.V.S.N. RANK BADGES
worn on the headgear
1935-38

1

3

4

5

1930-43

6

7

11

15

1. Comandante generale 3. Luogotenente generale 4. Console generale 5. Console
6. Primo seniore 7. Seniore 11. Aspirante 15. Primo capo squadra

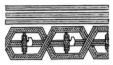

on the peaked cap 1938-43

1st Honorary corporal

Honorary corpora

ARM SHIELDS

M.V.S.N. H.Q.

B.S. Divisions (1935)

Black Shirts zones

Indep. Legion

B.S. Div. (1940)

PLATE 50

CAP BADGES

Generals

COLOURED CAP BANDS

Staff College

| Infantry | Cavalry | Artillery | Engineers | Chemical Warfare | Services |

COLLAR PATCHES

Tunic   Jacket   Greatcoat

Major, Artillery

RANK BADGES WORN ON COLLAR PATCHES

Generals   Senior commanders   Commanders   Junior commanders

PLATE 51

ARMY RANK BADGES (1935-40)

collar patches   on both forearms   collar patches

Tunic   Greatcoat   Greatcoat   Tunic

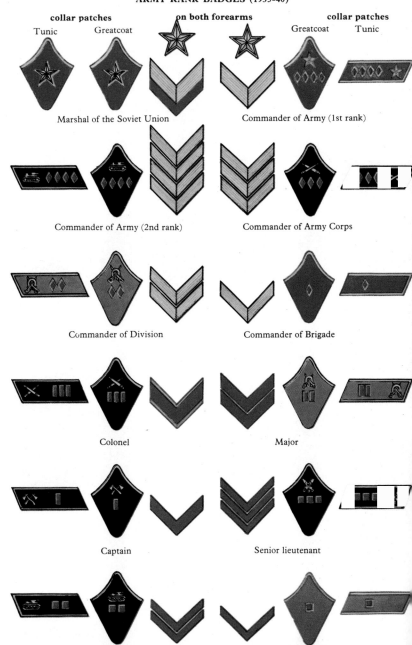

Marshal of the Soviet Union   Commander of Army (1st rank)

Commander of Army (2nd rank)   Commander of Army Corps

Commander of Division   Commander of Brigade

Colonel   Major

Captain   Senior lieutenant

Lieutenant   Junior lieutenant (1937)

PLATE 52

Political Personnel

Commissar of Army (1st rank)

Commissar of Army (2nd rank)

Commissar of Army Corps

Commissar of Division

Commissar of Brigade

Commissar of Regiment

Sleeve

Commissar of Battalion

Senior Politruk

Politruk

Junior politruk (1937)

PLATE 53

U.S.S.R.

Administrative Personnel

Intendant of Army

Intendant of Army Corps

Intendant of Division

Intendant of Brigade

Intendant 1st Class

Intendant 2nd Class

Intendant 3rd Class

Technician 1st Class

Technician 2nd Class (1937)

Technician 3rd class (1937)

Junior Commanders

Sergeant-major

Junior Platoon Co.

Section Co.

Private

PLATE 54

COLLAR BADGES
before 1936

Infantry

Border Guards

Cavalry

Machine Gunners

Artillery

Medical Dept.

Engineers

Camouflage

Signals

Veterinaries

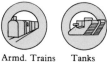

Railways

Drivers

Railways (Stations-Harbours)

Armd. Trains

Tanks

Armd. Cars

added in 1936

Medical

Band

Veterinaries

Commissariat

Armd. Troops

Legal

Administrative

Chemical

Technical Troops

Signals

PLATE 55

U.S.S.R.

Generals' cap badge

Marshal of the Soviet Union

General of the Army

Colonel-general

Major-general

Lieutenant-general

Colonel

Lieutenant-colonel

Major

Captain

PLATE 56

ARMY RANK BADGES (1940-43)

Senior lieutenant

Lieutenant

Junior lieutenant

Junior Commanders

Sergeant-major   Senior sergeant   Sergeant   Junior sergeant   Corporal

Kiev Tank School

Guards

Medical Department

PLATE 57

MARSHAL OF THE SOVIET UNION AND GENERALS

Parade Uniform (15.1.1943)

Marshal

Generals

Collars

Cuffs

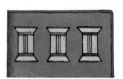

Generals' shoulder boards
(All uniforms except Field)

Marshal
of the Soviet Union

General of Army

Colonel-general

Lieutenant-general

Major-general

Greatcoat collar patches for Parade and Ordinary Uniforms

Marshal

Generals

PLATE 58

SENIOR COMMANDERS AND COMMANDERS
Collar Patches

Army (except Eng./Techn. staff) Engineer/Technical staff

 Senior commanders

 Commanders

Cuff Patches

Senior commanders  Commanders

Shoulder Boards

Colonel Lieutenant-colonel Major

Captain Senior lieutenant Lieutenant Junior lieutenant

ALL OTHER RANKS
Greatcoat Collar Patches

PLATE 59

MEDICAL, VETERINARY AND LEGAL SERVICES

Lawyer of Army Corps   Major-general   Lawyer 2nd Class   Lieutenant

Junior Commanders and Private

Sergeant-major   Senior sergeant   Sergeant   Junior sergeant   Corporal   Private

Army   Eng./Techn. Staff

Junior commanders   Private

Cadets

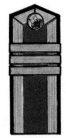

PLATE 60

FIELD UNIFORM

Colonel

Lieutenant-colonel

Major

Junior lieutenant

Captain

Senior lieutenant

Lieutenant

Junior lieutenant

Sergeant-major

Senior sergeant

Sergeant

Junior sergeant

Corporal

Private

O.R.'s belt buckle

wounded stripes

PLATE 61

U.S.S.R.

MARSHALS

Collar and cuff   4.2.1943

4.2.1943

Marshal of the Soviet Union   Artillery   Armour

SUPREME MARSHALS 27.10.1943

Artillery   Engineers   Signals   Armour

MARSHALS 27.10.1943

Engineers   Signals

PLATE 62

JUNIOR SOLDIERS SCHOOL
21.9.1943

Kalinski

Orlov

Stalingrad

Novo-Cherkask

ARTILLERY SPECIALISTS' SCHOOL
27.10.1943

MILITARY TRANSPORT

Cap band

Arm badge

PLATE 63

U.S.A.

CAP BADGES

Army Officers   West Point Academy   Transport Service   Harbour Boat Service

W.A.C.   Warrant Officers   U.S. Army Band

U.S. ARMY DIVERS' BREAST BADGES

Enlisted Men and W.A.C.   Master   1st class   2nd Class   Salvage

RANK BADGES

General of Army   General   Lieut.-general   Maj. general   Brigadier

Colonel   Lieut.-colonel   Major   Captain   1st Lieut.   2nd Lie

Chief warrant officer   Warrant officer

PLATE 64

NON-COMMISSIONED OFFICERS

First sergeant

Master sergeant

Technical sergeant

Staff sergeant

Technician
3rd grade

Sergeant

Technician
4th grade

Corporal

Technician 5th grade

Private 1st Class

Three-year
service stripe

U.S. ARMY MINE PLANTER SERVICE

Engineer

Master mine planter
or
Chief engineer

1st mate mine planter
or
Assistant engineer

2nd mate mine planter
or
2nd assistant engineer

Mine planter

PLATE 65

U.S.A.

OFFICERS' COLLAR BADGES

| Officer's U.S. | Engineers | Special Service | Signal C. | Unassigned officer | Field Artillery |

| Infantry | Military Police | Armd. Force | Tank Destroyer Force | Coast Art. | Cavalry |

| Band | Nat. Guard Bur. | General's aide | Transp. Corps | Gen. staff | Warrant officer | W.A. |

| Ordnance | Intelligence | A.F.N. | Quartermaster | Chemical Corps | Adjutant Corps | Finance |

| Physio-therapy | Judge advocate | Chaplains | Inspector G.S. | Hospital dietitian |

| Medical Corps | Contract surgeon | Sanitary Corps | Nurses Corps | Dental Corps | Pharmacy Corps | Vet. Corps | Med. Administr. |

BREAST BADGES

Combat infantryman

Gen. staff

Expert infantryman

Paratroops

Glider badge

PLATE 66

SHOULDER SLEEVE INSIGNIA
Army Groups

6th

12th

15th

Armies

1st

2nd

3rd

4th

5th

6th

7th

8th

9th

10th

15th

Army Corps

1st

2nd

3rd

4th

5th

6th

7th

8th

9th

10th

11th

12th

13th

14th

15th

16th

18th

19th

20th

21st

22nd

23rd

24th

36th

PLATE 67

SHOULDER SLEEVE INSIGNIA
Infantry and Airborne Divisions

 1st

 2nd

 3rd

 4th

 5th

 6th

 7th

 8th

 9th

 10th

 11th

 13th

 17th

24th

 25th

 26th

 27th

 28th

 29th

 30th

 31st

 32nd

 33rd

 34th

 35th

 36th

 37th

 38th

 39th

 40th

 41st

 42nd

 43rd

 44th

 45th

 63rd

 65th

 66th

 69th

 70th

 71st

 75th

PLATE 68

SHOULDER SLEEVE INSIGNIA
Infantry and Airborne Division

76th

77th

78th

79th

80th

81st

82nd

83rd

84th

85th

86th

87th

88th

89th

90th

91st

92nd

93rd

94th

95th

96th

97th

98th

99th

100th

101st

102nd

103rd

1st

104th

106th

Americal

2nd

Cavalry Divisions

3rd

21st

24th

56th

PLATE 69

U.S.A.

SHOULDER SLEEVE INSIGNIA

Cavalry Division

| 61st | 62nd | 63rd | 64th | 65th | 66th |

ARMY GROUND FORCES

Army Ground Forces   Replacement and School Command   General Hqs. Reserve   A.G.F. Replacement Depot   Army Service Forces   A.S.F. Training Center

Armd. Center   Airborne Command   A.A. Command   Amphibious Units   Ports of Embarkation

Engineer Amphibious Command   Army Specialized Training Program   A.S.T.P. (Reserve)   Tank Destroyer Units   Bomb Disposal personnel

Theaters

Pacific Ocean Area   European   European (Advance Base)   North African

South Atlantic   China-Burma-India   Middle East

PLATE 70

SHOULDER SLEEVE INSIGNIA
Headquarters

Allied Force Hqs.

S.H.A.E.F.

Hqs. South East Asia
Command

Base Commands

Iceland

Greenland

GHQ S.W. Pacific

Defense Commands

Southern

Eastern

London

Labrador, North-East
and Central Canada Command

Caribbean

Bermuda

Atlantic

Military District
of Washington

A.A. Art. Command
Western D.C.

A.A. Art. Command
Eastern D.C.

Pacific Coastal
F.D.S.

Chesapeake Bay
F.D.S.

Frontier Defense Sectors

A.A. Art. Command
Central D.C.

A.A. Art. Command
Southern D.C.

New England

N.Y.-Philadelphia   Southern Coastal

PLATE 71

U.S.A.

SHOULDER SLEEVE INSIGNIA
Service Commands

1st

North West

Persian Gulf

2nd

3rd

4th

5th

6th

7th

8th

9th

Departments

Alaskan

Antilles

Panama

Philippine

Hawaiian

MISCELLANEOUS U.S. UNITS

Combat Team
442

1st S.S.F.

Merrill's Marauders

Rangers

Task Fo

Chinese Combat
Training Command

French Forces
Training with
U.S. Troops

Allied Airborne

U.S. Military
Mission to Moscow

Veterans
Administration

Rangers

PLATE 72

SHOULDER SLEEVE INSIGNIA
Miscellaneous U.S. Units

Panama Hellgate

Hawaiian Separate
Coast Art. Bde.

Hawaiian Division

Hawaiian
Coastal
Défense

Philippine
Division

Amphib.
Training
Force 9

Aleutian
Islands

Officer's
Candidate School

Excellence
in
Artillery

Hawaiian
Nat'l guard

Filipino
Bn.

Army Hostesses

U.S. Military Academy
West Point

U.S. O. Camp Shows

Airborne Troops

Glider Borne Paratroops

Glider Borne Troops

Paratroops

PARATROOPS IDENTITY BACKGROUND OVALS

SLEEVE BADGES

W.W.1. Overseas
Chevrons—wounds

Meritorious
Service

Meritorious Awards

Overseas
Service Stripes

PLATE 73

GERMANY

OFFICERS' CAP BADGES (1, 2, 3) COLLAR (4, 5, 6, 7) AND CUFF (8, 9, 10) PATCHES

4

5

2

7

6

1

8

9

3

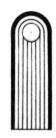

10

OFFICERS' RANK BADGES

Field-marshal	Colonel-general	General	Lieutenant-general	Major-general

Colonel	Lieutenant-colonel	Major	Captain	Lieutenant	2nd Lieutenant

PLATE 74

NON-COMMISSIONED OFFICERS AND OTHER RANKS

2

4

3

1

5

1. Cap badge   2, 3, 4. Collar patches   5. Cuff patch

Staff-sergeant   Sergeant-major   Sergeant   Lance-sergeant   N.C.O.

Staff-corporal   Corporal-major   Corporal-major   Corporal   Senior private
(over 6 years' service)

Privates' shoulder straps

PLATE 75

GERMANY

ARM BADGES (Except Mountain Guide)

| Sniper | *Jäger* | Standard-bearer | Mountain Troops | Mountain Guide |

| Helmsman | Signaller | Gunlayer | Smoke Troops operator |

| Defence Works | Medical Corps | Farriers | Artificer | radio-operator | Ordnance |

Harness/Motor Maintenance | Pigeoneer | Fortification Construction | Saddler cadet | Paymaster cadet | Fortification Maintenance

CUFF TITLES

PLATE 76

SHOULDER STRAPS BADGES

 Legal

 Anti-Tank

 Technical

 Reconnaissance

 Veterinary

 Administration

 Doctor

 Guards

 Ordnance

 Band

 Mot. Cyclist

 Mounted

 M.G. Bns.

 Observation

 Schools

 Art. Sch.

 M.G. Sch.

 Ord. Sch.

 War Sch.

 Physical Tr. Sch.

 Trainer Units

 Fortifications

 Tank Research

 N.C.O. Sch.

 Divisional H.Q.

 Frontier Defence

 Experimental Stations

 N.C.O. Sch.

 Army Corps H.Q.

 Observer Trainer

 O.R.'s belt buckle

 A.T. Trainer

PLATE 77

CLOSE COMBAT CLASP

GENERAL ASSAULT BADGES

General Assault

25–50

75–100

COMBAT BADGES

Infantry Assault

Army Parachutist

Army Balloon Observer

Army Anti-Aircraft

TANK BATTLE BADGES

Tank Battle

25–50

75–100

PLATE 78

TANK BATTLE BADGES

Marksman's badges (worn on lanyard)   Tank Marksman

Anti-Partisan

Destruction of a tank

Driver's Service

Military Police

Mountain Troops

Jäger

Mountain Troops

Destruction of an aircraft

Chaplain

Commemorative regimental badges

PLATE 79

GERMANY

ARM SHIELDS

WOUNDED BADGES

Spanish
Civil War

2nd W.W.

20.7.1944

PLATE 80

SCHUTZSTAFFEL

Cap Badges

Collar Patches

Arm Badge

Standard Bearer's Gorget

Officer's Belt Buckle

O.R.'s Belt Buckle

Cuff Titles

Adolf Hitler

SS-Polizei-Division

Hohenstaufen

Das Reich

PLATE 81

Germania

Deutschland

Der Führer

Reichsführer-SS

Totenkopf

30. Januar

Nord

Reinhard Heydrich

Nordland

Westland

Nordland

Westland

Götz von Berlichingen

Prinz Eugen

Florian Geyer

Wallonie

Theodor Eicke

Charlemagne

Frundsberg

PLATE 82

SCHUTZSTAFFEL

Collar Patches

5th   11th   13th   14th   15th

18th   19th   20th   21st

22nd   23rd   23rd–34th   25th

27th   28th   29th (Italian)   33rd

29th–30th (Russian)

36th   Indian   British

PLATE 83

OFFICER'S RANK BADGES

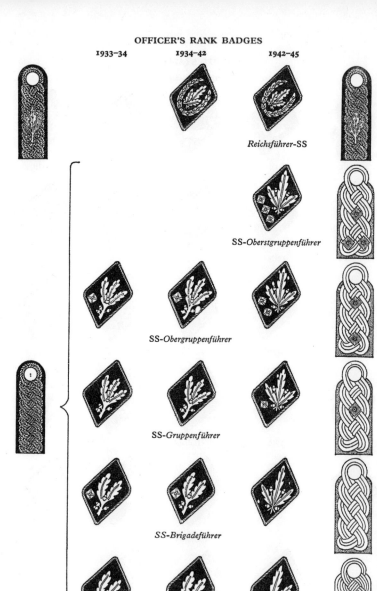

1933–34   1934–42   1942–45

Reichsführer-SS

SS-*Oberstgruppenführer*

SS-*Obergruppenführer*

SS-*Gruppenführer*

SS-*Brigadeführer*

SS-*Oberführer*

PLATE 84

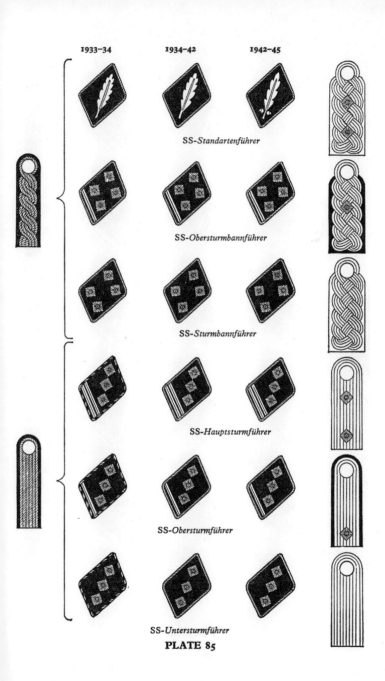

1933–34 1934–42 1942–45

SS-*Standartenführer*

SS-*Obersturmbannführer*

SS-*Sturmbannführer*

SS-*Hauptsturmführer*

SS-*Obersturmführer*

SS-*Untersturmführer*

PLATE 85

NON-COMMISSIONED OFFICERS

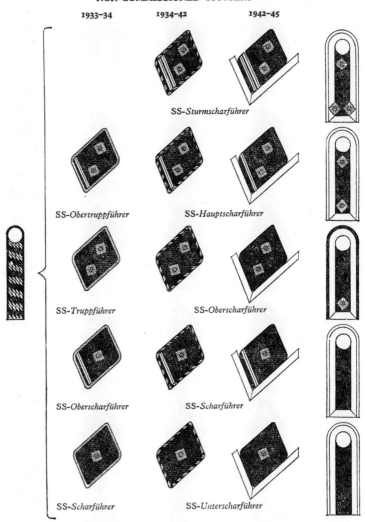

1933–34   1934–42   1942–45

SS-*Sturmscharführer*

SS-*Obertruppführer*   SS-*Hauptscharführer*

SS-*Truppführer*   SS-*Oberscharführer*

SS-*Oberscharführer*   SS-*Scharführer*

SS-*Scharführer*   SS-*Unterscharführer*

PLATE 86

OTHER RANKS

1933–34	1934–42	1942–45

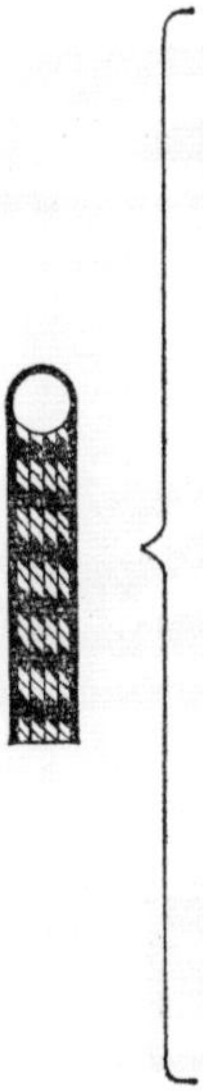

SS-*Rottenführer*

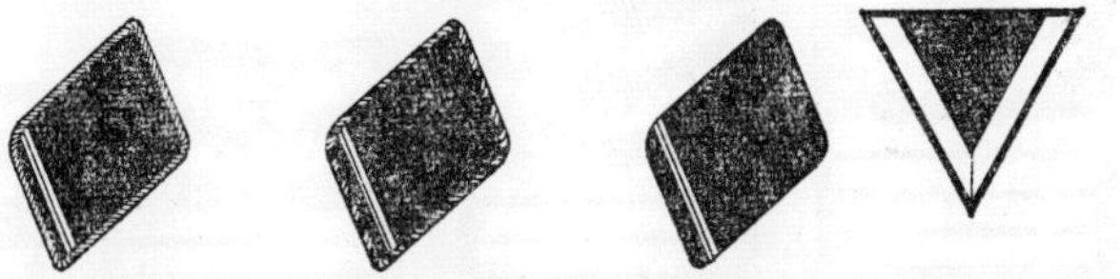

SS-*Sturmmann*

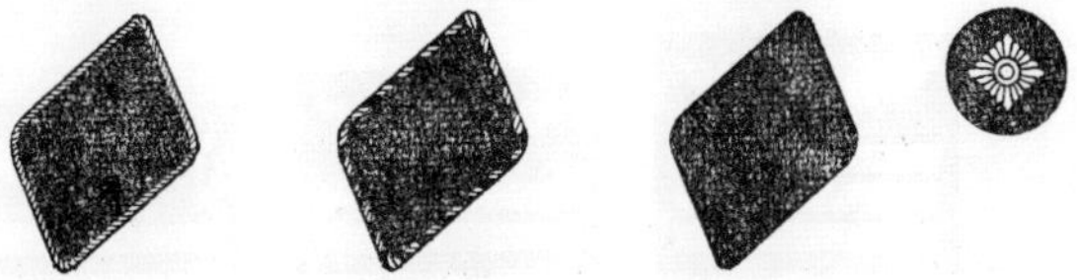

SS-*Mann(ober)*

SS-*Leibst. ADOLF HITLER*

DEUTSCHLAND

GERMANIA

DER FÜHRER

SS-*Stabsscharführer*

Alte Kämpfer

ex-Police

ex-Stahlhelm

PLATE 87

RANK BADGES FOR CAMOUFLAGE UNIFORMS

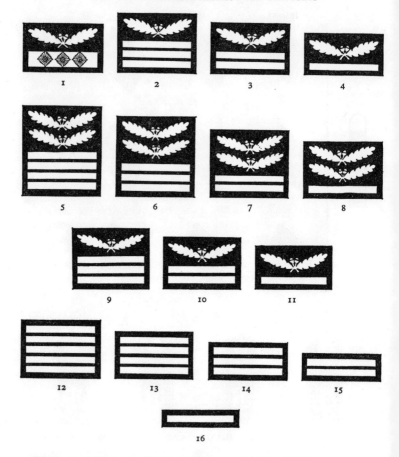

1. SS-*Oberstgruppenführer* 2. SS-*Obergruppenführer* 3. SS-*Gruppenführer* 4. SS-*Brigade-führer* 5. SS-*Oberführer* 6. SS-*Standartenführer* 7. SS-*Obersturmbannführer* 8. SS-*Sturm-bannführer* 9. SS-*Hauptsturmführer* 10. SS-*Obersturmführer* 11. SS-*Untersturmführer* 12. SS-*Sturmscharführer* 13. SS-*Hauptscharführer* 14. SS-*Oberscharführer* 15. SS-*Unter-scharführer* 16. SS-*Scharführer*

PLATE 88

Great Britain

In the second half of the seventeenth century, soldiers began to wear uniforms, the 'uniform' at first being confined to the coat, which was predominantly red. The soldier provided his own trousers and shoes, the choice of which was left to his discretion.

At that time the colonel 'owned' the regiment, and his emblem and colours were profusely displayed on the uniforms and standards.

Cromwell's New Model Army came into being in 1645 and was the first organised British Army. After the Restoration in 1661 it became the Standing Army, the forefather of the Regular Army.

Red remained the colour of the infantryman's coat for two centuries, with the exception of the Rifle regiments, when they were eventually formed, who wore 'rifle green'. The Royal Engineers wore red coats, and red or blue coats were worn by the various cavalry regiments. The Royal Artillery and service branches of the Army adopted blue uniforms.

In 1751, a Royal Warrant ended the wearing of the colonels' emblems, and replaced them with proper regimental 'devices', as badges were then called. Some of these 'devices' are still worn nowadays. At the same time uniforms became standardised, and the above was the first of a long series of royal warrants and precise 'Dress' regulations.

Khaki uniforms were worn for the first time during the Indian Mutiny and were then white uniforms, roughly dyed, in order to make the soldiers less conspicuous. The word 'khaki' is derived from Urdu and means 'dusty'.

In later campaigns, for instance during the Afghan War, uniforms were again dyed, but it was only during the Boer wars that the adoption of a camouflaged uniform became imperative, because of the guerilla nature of the war. Khaki was adopted as a standard uniform, to be worn at all stations abroad, except Canada. In 1902, a khaki service dress for all ranks was introduced and its colour proved most suitable for the trench warfare of World War 1. During this war the steel helmet, as we know it, was adopted and, though modified, its design is practically the same today.

World War 1 marked the end of an era, and with it the coloured uniforms also disappeared. Khaki service dress became standard issue, although a blue 'walking out' uniform was chosen in 1936 for the Coronation. The year after, the famous khaki battledress was introduced, together with its appropriate webbing equipment. The headdress was a helmet or the khaki field cap, the latter later being substituted with a beret. The black beret was already worn by the regiments of the Royal Armoured Corps, with the exception of the 11th Hussars who wore a brown beret with a scarlet band. The Airborne Forces wore maroon berets and Commandos and Reconnaissance Corps wore green berets. The rest of the Army was issued with khaki berets.

Battledress was made of khaki serge, and was composed of a tunic or blouse buttoned onto the trousers, the trousers being tucked into the webbing anklets. Variations of battledress tunics can be divided into two types: a smart lined tunic, with all buttons hidden by flaps, and another type with all the buttons showing and normally of a shabbier appearance.

Collar badges were worn on the service dress together with metal shoulder titles on the shoulder straps. New types of identification badges were introduced for the battledress.

In 1940 some coloured felt strips (2 in. $\times$ $\frac{1}{4}$ in.) were adopted on the sleeves, to be worn below the formation sign. Nineteen in all, the colours of these strips were as follows:

scarlet	Infantry (except Rifle regiments)
rifle green	Rifle regiments
purple	Royal Army Chaplains Department
red	Corps of Military Police
green	Intelligence Corps
yellow	Royal Army Pay Corps
Cambridge blue	Army Educational Corps
dull cherry	Royal Army Medical Corps
red–blue	Royal Artillery
blue–red	Royal Engineers
yellow–red	Royal Armoured Corps
yellow–blue	Royal Army Service Corps
blue–white	Royal Signals
green–white	Army Dental Corps
red–green	Pioneer Corps
grey–yellow	Army Catering Corps
red–blue–red	Royal Army Ordnance Corps
red–yellow–blue	Royal Electrical and Mechanical Engineers
black–red–black	Army Physical Training Corps

At about the same time, cloth shoulder titles replaced brass ones and were stitched at the top of the sleeves, just below the seam. They were printed, or embroidered, on coloured felts and, as well as showing the corps or regimental title, they also showed the arm or corps colour.

Infantry regiments (with the exception of Rifle regiments) wore shoulder titles with white lettering on scarlet (QUEEN'S, BUFFS, BEDFS. and HERTS., CAMERONIANS, INNISKILLING, LOYALS, NORTH STAFFORD, DURHAM L.I. etc.). Black and red lettering on 'rifle green' were the shoulder titles of the Rifle Brigade and the K.R.R.C. As in the days of full dress, the former wore green jackets with black piping, the latter green jackets with red piping.

Guards regiments wore shoulder titles in their regimental colours. The Royal Artillery title was in red lettering on a blue background. The Royal Army Ordnance Corps wore the letters R.A.O.C. in blue on red, and the Royal Army Medical Corps R.A.M.C. in white on dull cherry background, and so on.

Some regiments had shoulder titles made abroad and they were not made in the correct colours. For instance, the Duke of Wellington's Regiment, whose shoulder titles were made in Italy, are embroidered on 'flame red' instead of on scarlet.

The cavalry regiments formed part of the Royal Armoured Corps and wore its shoulder title. However, regimental cavalry shoulder titles exist, such as that of the 17/21 LANCERS, embroidered in white on black cloth.

The outbreak of World War 2 caught the British soldier in the colonies wearing the khaki drill service dress, the 'summer' version of the service dress worn at home. Regimental patches were worn on the left side of the colonial helmet on the puggree.

Khaki drill shorts were worn with hose and puttees and, although the uniform was basically the same for both officers and other ranks, that of the former was often made with better cloth, was better tailored and the collar was opened to show the shirt and tie.

Plate 1. Cap Badges and Gorget Patches

The cap badge worn by field-marshals was, and still is, composed of crossed batons on a wreath of laurel, surmounted by the Royal Crest. That of general, lieutenant-general and major-general carries a crossed baton and sword in the centre instead of crossed batons. Brigadier-generals wore the Royal Crest, which was also worn by officers belonging to the Extra-Regimentally Employed List, formed by officers of the judge advocate's staff, staff quartermasters and quartermasters employed on staff and administrative duties.

The gorget patches trace their origin to the metal gorget worn on the chest by officers until about 1830. Previously the gorget was that part of the armour meant to protect the upper chest and the throat of the wearer. The armour slowly went into disuse, but the gorget remained as a symbol of rank in the form of a crescent-shaped, embossed plate, hung around the neck by means of ribbons. Gorget patches were later introduced in

India and, as we know them today, were brought in in 1896. They were later applied on the collar of the service dress.

Field-marshals and generals wore scarlet gorget patches with gold leaves and acorns embroidered along the centre. They were substituted by a gold gimp on the patches worn on the battledress or shirt collar.

Gold leaves and acorns used to be the distinctive ornament of field-marshals and general officers, widely embroidered on the collars, cuffs and on the back flaps of the skirts of the red tunic.

The gorget patches of brigadiers and substantive colonels were made of scarlet cloth with a red gimp. Those for battledress were 2 in. long. The gorget patch button is a smaller version of that worn on the tunic.

Officers' Rank Badges

During the present century the British officers' rank badges did not change a great deal, except for the rank of 2nd lieutenant who, at the beginning of the century, had no star: a lieutenant wore only one star, and a captain two stars. The rank badges illustrated are those commonly known during World War 2; worn on the shoulders from the 1880s, they were basically a composition of three different badges, i.e. the crossed baton and sword, the crown and the star.

Subalterns wore stars; majors wore a crown, and a star was added under the crown for each superior rank. Brigadier-generals wore three stars and a crown. A crossed baton and a sword and a star is the distinctive badge of major-generals, the crown replacing the star for that of lieutenant-generals. Generals had both crown and star over a crossed baton and sword. Field-marshals wore the crossed batons on a laurel wreath, with a crown above.

The star is also called a 'pip', and there are several different types, for instance those worn by Guards regiments, and the black stars and crowns worn by Rifle regiments.

A great variety of crowns and pips can be found nowadays, made in wire embroidery, in gilt and enamel, brass, blackened brass, plastic, anodised metal and worsted, or in bronze for service dress. All these types are in different sizes. The crowns, of course, followed the pattern in use at the time: the Victorian crown until 1902; the Imperial or Kings' crown as it was worn in the reigns of Edward VII, George V, Edward VIII and George VI, until in 1953 Elizabeth II adopted St. Edward's crown, commonly known as the Queen's crown.

The rank badges worn on the battledress were normally of the worsted type in buff and brown thread, machine embroidered, flat or protruding, on a cardboard backing.

Though there are types embroidered on khaki material, others have been embroidered on coloured felts and are listed below:

red	General Staff
	Royal Artillery
	Royal Army Ordnance Corps
	Military Police
	Pioneer Corps
	Royal Electrical and Mechanical Engineers
scarlet	Infantry (except L.I. and Rifle regiments)
royal blue	Royal Engineers
Cambridge blue	Army Educational Corps
rifle green	Rifle regiments
dark green	Light Infantry regiments
emerald green	Army Dental Corps
yellow	Royal Armoured Corps
	Royal Army Service Corps
	Royal Army Pay Corps
dull cherry	Royal Army Medical Corps
beech brown	Women's Royal Army Corps
purple	Royal Army Chaplains Department
maroon	Parachute Regiment
	Royal Army Veterinary Corps
grey	Army Catering Corps

Plate 2. Warrant Officers' and Non-commissioned Officers' Rank Badges

Warrant officers wore, and still wear, their rank badges on both forearms of the jacket or tunic, over the cuffs.

Regimental sergeant-majors and superintending clerks of the Foot Guards wear a badge depicting the Royal Arms in full colour embroidered on khaki material (1).

Staff sergeant-majors (1st Class) and conductors wear a smaller badge representing the Royal Arms partly surrounded by a wreath of laurel (2).

This and all the following rank badges could either be thread-embroidered or made in brass.

Regimental corporal-majors and farriers corporal-majors of the Household Cavalry and warrant officers (1st Class) wear the Royal Arms surrounded by a coloured border (3).

Regimental quartermaster-corporals and farriers quartermaster-corporals of the Household Cavalry, regimental quartermaster-sergeants, and Orderly Room quartermaster-sergeants of the Foot Guards wear a crown surrounded by a laurel wreath (4).

Squadron corporal-majors of the Life Guards wear a crown 1½ in. wide (5). Squadron corporal-majors of the Royal Horse Guards and warrant officers (2nd Class) of other corps and regiments wear a crown 2 in. wide (5).

Warrant officers and N.C.O.s of the Household Cavalry did not use the rank title of 'sergeant', because it is derived from the Latin verb 'servire' (to serve). They replaced it with that of 'corporal'.

Warrant officers of the Royal Artillery are called 'master gunner' respectively of the 1st, 2nd and 3rd class, and wear a gun similar to that in the cap badge, on the forearms below the rank badge; a brass gun if the badge is made in brass, worsted if the badge is worsted.

Bandmasters wear a lyre set on a wreath of oak leaves and surmounted by a crown on both forearms. The same badge, but smaller, is worn by non-commissioned officers and musicians of the military bands, over the rank chevrons or on its own on the right upper sleeve.

Squadron quartermaster-corporals and staff corporals of the Household Cavalry wear four chevrons, pointing upward, below a crown on both forearms (6), drum-majors the same chevrons below a drum (7). Following the same pattern, bugle-majors wear a bugle over the chevrons, and trumpet-majors two crossed trumpets. A crown over the trumpets is worn in the case of a trumpet-major of the Household Cavalry. All the chevrons listed below are worn with points downwards on the upper arm of both sleeves.

Corporals-of-horse of the Household Cavalry, Squadron, Battery and Company quartermaster-sergeants, colour sergeants and staff sergeants, all wear three chevrons below a crown (8).

Other badges can be worn above the chevrons: a gun by sergeants of the Royal Artillery, the engineers' grenade by sergeants of the Royal Engineers, a red flaming grenade by sergeants of the Grenadier Guards and the figure of Mercury by sergeants of the Royal Corps of Signals.

Band sergeants wear the lyre above their chevrons, except for band sergeants (and band corporals) of the Foot Guards who do not wear the badge.

Corporals of the Royal Artillery are called 'bombardiers' and, together with corporals and band corporals of the Foot Guards, wear two chevrons (11).

Band bombardiers, band corporals (except Foot Guards) and lance-corporals of the band and bugles of the Durham Light Infantry wear the lyre above the two chevrons.

The Household Cavalry and Foot Guards have no one-chevron rank as their lance-corporals wear two chevrons. The two-chevron rank of the Household Cavalry has a crown above (10). The lance-corporals and lance-bombardiers of the rest of the Army wear only one chevron (12), with a lyre in the case of band lance-corporals or band lance-bombardiers.

Formation Signs (*Pl. 3–4 also Pl. 13–14*).

The British Army adopted formation signs during World War 1 in order to provide an easy form of visual identification of the various units. These signs were worn on the uniform sleeve and painted on vehicles, road signs, etc. As this information was given by a symbol, the formation sign had the advantage of not disclosing its meaning to an outsider. Each unit was proud of its own formation sign and became very attached to it. It went some way to creating an *esprit de corps*.

After World War 1, the use of formation signs was discontinued, although most Territorials continued wearing their divisional signs until, at the beginning of World War 2, their use was officially reintroduced throughout the Army.

The symbolic meaning of a formation sign is usually connected with the unit it represents, although sometimes in rather obscure ways. The symbol was normally chosen by the personnel of the unit.

There are several types of formation sign: mechanically printed in colour on material, mechanically embroidered on coloured felt and, in certain cases, hand embroidered and woven.

Other types in existence were made by the soldiers themselves in occupied countries during World War 1 and World War 2. And there must be many examples made by keen collectors.

Although the design of the badge is always the same there are often variations of colours: the 'HD' of the 51st (Highland) Division, for instance, could be found in red, yellow or brown. Generally speaking, the details of most signs do not necessarily look the same.

Plate 3. Supreme Headquarters, British and Allied Forces

The formation sign of G.H.Q. Home Forces was represented by a winged lion set on a round red and blue background, with two yellow frames. The Star of India, on the same background but rectangular in this case, was the badge of G.H.Q. India. The badges of the Allied Forces H.Q. (Algiers and Naples), Supreme Headquarters Allied Expeditionary Forces (north-western Europe), Supreme Allied Command, south-east Asia, and H.Q. 15th Army Group were worn both by American and British troops, the latter composed of 8th British and 5th U.S. Armies in Italy. The S.H.A.E.F. badge shows the crusader's sword alight in the 'darkness' of German-occupied Europe, the sword pointing to the rainbow of peace.

The sign of Allied Land Forces, South-East Asia, was in fact never issued to U.S. forces. American-issued badges are heavily silk woven and can easily be recognised. H.Q. 21st Army Group commanded the 2nd British Army and the 1st Canadian Army.

At the time of the Ardennes battle, the 1st and 9th U.S. Armies came under the operational command of 21st Army Group, the 1st for only a month (16 December, 1944–16 January, 1945), the 9th until 3 April, 1945.

The Headquarters 21st Army Group was formed from G.H.Q. Home Forces and initially had its quarters at St. Paul's School, West Kensington.

The assault forces who landed in Normandy on 6 June, 1944, were the 2nd British and 1st U.S. Armies, under the command of Field-Marshal Montgomery. Subsequently the British forces were grouped into 21st Army Group, and the Americans into 12th Army Group.

On 1 September, 1944, General Eisenhower established his head-quarters (S.H.A.E.F.) in France, taking direct command of all operations in that sector. Thus Field-Marshal Montgomery was the commander of 21st Army Group only.

The sign of Central Mediterranean Force symbolises the 'torch of liberty' being brought from over the sea.

Armies

The 1st and 2nd Armies wore a similar formation sign: the crusader's shield and sword, with a red cross on the shield for the 1st and a blue cross for the 2nd Army. The 1st Army invaded North Africa during the winter 1942–43, while the 2nd Army, formed in England in the summer of 1943, landed in Normandy and took part in the whole north-western European campaign.

The 8th Army was formed in Egypt in 1941 from the existing Army of the Nile. The first occasion its name appeared in print was when General Sir Alan Cunningham was appointed as its commander, on 18 November, 1941, although it was officially known as such from about 26 September.

It fought in the North African campaign, from El Alamein to Tunis, took part in the invasion of Sicily and, together with the 5th U.S. Army, slowly crept up the Italian peninsula, reaching Austria by the beginning of May, 1945.

The 9th Army was formed in the Levant, at the rear of the 8th Army, and was commanded by General Sir Henry M. Wilson. He was nick-named 'Jumbo', a fact which influenced the design of the Army's badge.

A yellow Assyrian lion was adopted as the sign of the 10th Army that was formed in Iraq in 1941 at the time of the rebellion and controlled Syria, Iraq and Persia.

The Burmese dragon was the symbolic animal chosen for the badge of the 12th Army, raised in Burma on 28 May, 1945, that together with the 14th Army was to retake Burma and Malaya from the Japanese. The 14th Army was the formation that for years withstood the Japanese armies.

Army Corps

In September, 1939, the British Expeditionary Force was sent to France. Originally it was composed of the 1st and 2nd Corps deployed between the 1st and the 7th French Armies, the latter supporting the Belgians who were supposed to defend the area between Louvain and Antwerp in case of retreat. The spearhead design of the 1st Corps was adopted because it was the 'first' Corps of the Army. The formation sign of the 2nd Corps was chosen after the name of its commander, Lieutenant-General Sir Alan Brooke. In March, 1940, the B.E.F. had been strengthened by an additional Corps, the 3rd, whose badge was a fig leaf, after the name of its commander, Lieutenant-General Sir Ronald Adam.

The 4th Corps was part of the 14th Army, together with the 15th, the 33rd and later the 34th Indian Corps.

The 5th Corps took part in the Norwegian expedition in 1940, hence the choice of a Viking ship as its badge. Later it joined the 1st Army and took part in the North African campaign. It landed in Sicily and, as part of the 8th Army, fought its way all along the Italian peninsula.

The charging knight of the 8th Corps was adopted in February, 1943 as it was composed of two armoured divisions. It landed in Normandy and subsequently took part in the operations, reaching the River Elbe in the spring of 1945.

The 9th Corps saw active service in North Africa with the 1st Army. It wore two formation signs: the black cat in connection with the cat's reputed nine lives and a white trumpet with nine white squares on its banner.

The 8th Army was originally formed by the 13th and 30th Corps, the gazelle becoming the badge of the former during its connection with the desert. The 13th Corps remained with the 8th Army and, at the end of the war, occupied north-east Italy, while early in 1944, the 30th Corps, then formed by the 50th (Northumbrian), 51st (Highland) and 7th (Armoured) Divisions, returned to Britain to join the 2nd Army in training for the invasion of Europe.

The 10th Corps was formed before the battle of El Alamein. Heavily armoured, it had been concentrated behind the lines and was employed in the breakthrough operation in the sector of the 30th Corps.

The 11th Corps served as part of the Home Forces and was later disbanded in Britain before it had seen active service overseas.

The 12th Corps, together with the 1st, 8th and 30th Corps, belonged to the 2nd Army and fought in France, Belgium, Holland and Germany. Its formation sign with an oak, an ash and a thorn in an oval on a black background was chosen as a link with the name of its commander, Major-General Sir A. F. A. N. Thorne and with 'the Oak, the Ash and the Thorn', in *Puck of Pook's Hill* by Rudyard Kipling, the Corps having been raised in the Pook's Hill country.

The 25th Corps had a red lion on a yellow rectangular background, formerly the badge of the Headquarters of British Troops in Cyprus.

Plate 4. Armoured Divisions

The Guards Armoured Division was raised in September, 1941, and it adopted the formation sign of the Guards Division of World War 1. It landed in Normandy and took an active part in the campaign in north-western Europe.

The 1st Armoured Division fought with the B.E.F. in France in 1940 and, after refitting in Britain, it was sent to the Middle East towards the end of 1941. Later, during the same campaign, together with the 10th Armoured Division, it formed the 10th Army Corps, which drove from El Alamein to Tunisia. As part of the 8th Army it fought in the Italian campaign and in 1945 it was broken up, although its 2nd Armoured Brigade continued wearing its formation sign. The rhinoceros was an appropriate divisional badge and a variation of it, a charging rhinoceros, was worn during the latter campaign.

A fox's mask was the sign of the 10th Armoured Division, as it was originally formed of mechanised cavalry and yeomanry units.

The 2nd Armoured Division was sent to the Middle East in November, 1940; a plumed white knight's helmet on a red background was its badge.

The 6th Armoured Division, with the clenched mailed gauntlet sign, served in North Africa with the 1st Army and was later assigned to the 8th Army. It fought in the Italian campaign and reached Gorizia in the north-east by the beginning of May, 1945.

The 7th is the best known of the armoured divisions. It was formed in Egypt in 1938 as a mobile division based near Mersa Matruh. In December, 1939, the division became known as the 7th Armoured Division and its commander, Major-General O'Moore Creagh, adopted the well-known jerboa divisional sign. When later the division was employed in north-western Europe a new sign was adopted, the red jerboa, now picked out in white, on a black rectangular background.

The formation sign of the 8th Armoured Division depicted a traffic light set on the word 'GO' on a green background. This division was sent to the Middle East but was split up soon after its arrival.

The 9th Armoured Division was formed in 1941 and was employed as a training formation until it was disbanded in 1944. Its badge was a black and white panda's head. It is said that this badge was chosen with reference to the division's training role, as the panda, although a species of bear, is not a fierce animal.

Another division raised in 1941 was the 11th Armoured which chose the badge of a charging bull; it landed in Normandy and subsequently fought through France, Belgium, Holland and Germany.

The 42nd Armoured Division was formed by the conversion to armour of the 42nd (East Lancashire) Division. It did not see active service and was disbanded in 1943, its engineers later becoming part of the 79th Armoured Division. As an infantry formation, the 42nd (East Lancashire) Division joined the B.E.F. in France, and took part in the retreat from Dunkirk.

Major-General Sir Percy C. S. Hobart dedicated his life to the assertion of armour as the strength of a modern army. He was the creator of the 7th Armoured Division, later of the 11th Armoured Division, and perhaps his masterpiece was the 76th Armoured Division that he actually commanded until its disbandment in 1945. Initially it was raised as a normal armoured division, but soon after it was trained to handle all sorts of armoured implements, such as amphibious tanks, mine-sweeping tanks and bridging tanks. Other machines laid flexible carpets over soft ground, others carried projectors capable of illuminating the battlefield. Churchill VII tanks were fitted with flame-thrower equipment called 'Crocodile'. They became known as Churchill Crocodile tanks and were extensively used in the north-west European campaign. All these strange-looking tanks became collectively known as 'Funnies'.

Armoured Brigades

The 4th and 7th Armoured Brigades, together with a support group, initially formed the 7th Armoured Division, and were thus entitled to wear the jerboa badge.

The 4th Armoured Brigade was later transferred to Britain and took part in the invasion of Europe, while the 7th was transferred to Burma in 1942 where it adopted the green 'Jungle rat' as its badge. By 1944 the 7th Armoured Brigade was again part of the 8th Army, now on the Italian front.

The fox's mask of the 8th Armoured Brigade obviously originates from the formation sign of the 10th Armoured Division. The Brigade was employed in north-western Europe and so was the 6th Guards Tank Brigade, that was originally part of the Guards Armoured Division.

A white horse on a rectangular or semi-circular green background was the badge of the 9th Armoured Brigade; the horse was chosen because the brigade was formed by cavalry and yeomanry regiments.

The armour-clad horse's head, in white on a black background, served as the badge of the 20th Armoured Brigade. A red devil seen peeping from behind two blue triangles was that of the 16th Armoured Brigade.

The 22nd Armoured Brigade, with the stag's head sign, was composed of yeomanry regiments and served initially with the 8th Army, moving later to north-western Europe.

The 23rd Armoured Brigade was raised in Liverpool and naturally chose the liver bird for its badge. It fought in North Africa and Italy with the 8th Army and later it was despatched to Greece to quell the E.L.A.S. rising. The badge could be either round or square.

The 25th Armoured Engineer Brigade was a special unit for tank support; it took part in the Italian campaign.

The badge of the 27th Armoured Brigade depicted a sea-horse and, together with the 34th Armoured Brigade, it belonged to the 21st Army Group.

Two triangles, one inverted above the other, was a common emblem among armoured and tank units and was called a 'diabolo'. The 31st Independent Armoured Brigade wore a pale green diabolo. The 33rd and 35th Armoured Brigades instead wore equilateral triangles: the former green and black, the latter brown and green.

Army Tank Brigades

Army Tank Brigades wore diabolos composed of isosceles triangles. The 21st Army Tank Brigade initially wore a yellow diabolo, later changing to a black one on a yellow-red shield.

The 23rd Army Tank Brigade wore a green diabolo, the 24th blue and the 25th black with a small white maple leaf to commemorate its association with the 1st Canadian Division.

The 36th Tank Brigade's badge was a red and a black triangle.

The 1st Armoured Replacement Group C.M.F. supplied and refitted all armoured units of the 8th Army in Italy.

Its badge showed the head of Mars on a background of R.A.C. colours: yellow and red.

Cap Badges (*Pl. 5–12*)

Traditionally the headdress of the British soldier always displays the emblem of the unit to which he belongs: battalion badges were even issued to the Volunteer and Territorial units. The metal cap badge, as we know it, is derived from the helmet plate and was brought into general use towards the end of the last century.

Different cap badges were worn on different headdresses and although the officers and 'other ranks' badges were generally similar, those of the former were made of superior metals, i.e. gilt instead of brass, silver plate or silver instead of white metal. In some cases coloured enamels embellished the officer's cap badge. Officers have also worn bronzed badges with 'service dress' and, in the cavalry regiments particularly, many wore gold and silver embroidered badges as well.

In 1941 plastic badges were issued to most of the army with the exception of the cavalry regiments. They were in three colours: grey, pale fawn and brown.

Only 'other ranks' cap badges of the Regular Army, as worn during World War 2, are illustrated in this volume. When the officer's badge differs in design from that of the 'other ranks' a full description is given.

Plate 5. Cavalry and Armoured Regiments
The titles should be read from left to right and from top to bottom:

The Life Guards
Royal Horse Guards (The Blues)
1st King's Dragoon Guards
The Queen's Bays (2nd Dragoon Guards)
3rd Carabiniers (Prince of Wales's Dragoon Guards)
4th/7th Royal Dragoon Guards
5th Royal Inniskilling Dragoon Guards
1st The Royal Dragoons
The Royal Scots Greys (2nd Dragoons)
3rd The King's Own Hussars
4th Queen's Own Hussars
7th Queen's Own Hussars
8th King's Royal Irish Hussars
   Officers had the Harp between the Royal Crest and the roman
   numeral VIII. A scroll below reads: *Pristinae Virtutis Memores.*
9th Queen's Royal Lancers
10th Royal Hussars (Prince of Wales's Own)
11th Hussars (Prince Albert's Own)

Plate 6. Cavalry and Armoured Regiments
12th Royal Lancers (Prince of Wales's)
13th/18th Royal Hussars (Queen Mary's Own)
14th/20th King's Hussars
15th/19th The King's Royal Hussars
16th/5th The Queen's Royal Lancers
17th/21st Lancers
22nd Dragoons
23rd Hussars
24th Lancers
25th Dragoons
26th Hussars
27th Lancers
Royal Tank Regiment
Royal Armoured Corps
Reconnaissance Corps

Before April, 1939, the Royal Tank Regiment was called the Royal Tank Corps and, in that month, together with the mechanised cavalry regiments, it became part of the Royal Armoured Corps. The latter initially wore a cap badge depicting the letters 'RAC' within a laurel wreath; the badge illustrated was adopted in 1941.

The Reconnaissance Corps was raised in January, 1941, and in December, 1943, it also became part of the R.A.C. The Reconnaissance units of the 49th (West Riding) Division wore a small, white metal Yorkshire rose superimposed in the centre of the cap badge; Scottish units wore a Scottish lion on a circular tablet in the centre of the badge.

Plate 7. Corps, Administrative Departments, etc.

Royal Regiment of Artillery
Royal Horse Artillery
Honourable Artillery Company (Artillery and Infantry)
Corps of Royal Engineers
Royal Army Service Corps
Royal Corps of Signals
Royal Army Ordnance Corps
Royal Army Medical Corps
Corps of Military Police
Military Provost Staff Corps
Royal Army Veterinary Corps
Army Air Corps
Army Dental Corps
Royal Electrical and Mechanical Engineers
Intelligence Corps

Plate 8. Corps, Administrative Departments, etc.

Royal Army Pay Corps
Army Physical Training Corps
Pioneer Corps
Army Educational Corps
General Service Corps
Army Catering Corps (unassigned troops)
General Service Corps (training units)
Parachute Regiment

The Intelligence Corps, the Army Physical Training Corps and the Pioneer Corps were formed in 1940, although the latter also existed during World War 1. The Royal Electrical and Mechanical Engineers came into being in 1942, and so did the General Service Corps. The second cap badge of the G.S.C. was adopted in 1944 to be worn by G.S.C. personnel engaged in infantry training.

All ranks of the Parachute Regiment and the Glider Pilot Regiment wore the Army Air Corps badge, of which they were part. In May, 1943, a new cap badge was approved for the Parachute Regiment.

Foot Guards
Grenadier Guards:
> Warrant officers, orderly room sergeants, sergeants, band sergeants and musicians wore a crowned Royal Cypher on the ball of the grenade.

Coldstream Guards:
> The Star of the Order of the Garter in oval shape for officers, round shape for the other ranks.

Scots Guards

Irish Guards

Welsh Guards

The cap badges of the Warrant officers and some N.C.O. ranks of the Foot Guards regiments were often made with different metals to distinguish them from the officers and other ranks.

Plate 9. Infantry of the Line
Hackles and special badges awarded to regiments in Plates 9–12 have been mentioned whenever they were worn.

The Royal Scots (The Royal Regiment)
> The officer's cap badge was diamond-shaped, with the thistle in the centre, in gilt on green enamel, surrounded by a circle inscribed *Nemo Me Impune Lacessit*.

The Queen's Royal Regiment (West Surrey)

The Buffs (Royal East Kent Regiment)

The King's Own Royal Regiment (Lancaster)

The Royal Northumberland Fusiliers—with red hackle

The Royal Warwickshire Regiment

The Royal Fusiliers (City of London Regiment)—white hackle
> Officers: gilt grenade and crown with a silver rose in the centre and a small silver horse below the Garter.

The King's Regiment (Liverpool)

The Royal Norfolk Regiment

The Lincolnshire Regiment
> Officers: a diamond-cut, eight-pointed star in silver with silver sphinx on 'EGYPT', on blue background, surrounded by a gilt circle inscribed: 'Lincolnshire Regiment'.

The Devonshire Regiment

The Suffolk Regiment

The Somerset Light Infantry (Prince Albert's)

The West Yorkshire Regiment (The Prince of Wales's Own)
The East Yorkshire Regiment (The Duke of York's Own)
The Bedfordshire and Hertfordshire Regiment

Plate 10. Infantry of the Line

The Leicestershire Regiment
The Green Howards (Alexandra, Princess of Wales's Own Yorkshire
   Regiment)
The Lancashire Fusiliers—primrose yellow hackle
The Royal Scots Fusiliers—white hackle
The Cheshire Regiment
The Royal Welch Fusiliers—white hackle
   Officers wore forage cap and beret badges in gold embroidery with
   a silver dragon on the ball of the grenade.
The South Wales Borderers
The King's Own Scottish Borderers—white and black cock feathers
The Cameronians (Scottish Rifles)—black hackle
The Royal Inniskilling Fusiliers—grey hackle
The Gloucestershire Regiment—back badge
The Worcestershire Regiment—valise star
The East Lancashire Regiment
The East Surrey Regiment
The Duke of Cornwall's Light Infantry—red feathers
The Duke of Wellington's Regiment (West Riding)

Plate 11. Infantry of the Line

The Border Regiment
The Royal Sussex Regiment
   Although the officers' badge is very similar to that of the other ranks,
   the details of its design are entirely different.
The Hampshire Regiment
   Officers: a silver eight-pointed star with crowned Garter in the
   centre. The Hampshire red rose within the Garter and the regi-
   mental title on a scroll just below.
The South Staffordshire Regiment
The Dorsetshire Regiment
The South Lancashire Regiment (The Prince of Wales's Volunteers)
The Welch Regiment
The Black Watch (Royal Highland Regiment)—red hackle
The Oxfordshire and Buckinghamshire Light Infantry
The Essex Regiment
The Sherwood Foresters (Nottinghamshire and Derbyshire Regiment)
The Loyal Regiment (North Lancashire)

The Northamptonshire Regiment

The Royal Berkshire Regiment (Princess Charlotte of Wales's)
   Officers: The China dragon below a crown in silver, on three coils of
   rope in bronze.

The Queen's Own Royal West Kent Regiment

The King's Own Yorkshire Light Infantry—green pompon

The King's Shropshire Light Infantry

Plate 12. Infantry of the Line

The Middlesex Regiment (The Duke of Cambridge's Own)

The King's Royal Rifle Corps—black badge

The Wiltshire Regiment (Duke of Edinburgh's)
   Officers' badges have no coronet nor scroll, and are in silver with gilt
   cypher.

The Manchester Regiment

The North Staffordshire Regiment (The Prince of Wales's)

The York and Lancaster Regiment

The Durham Light Infantry

The Highland Light Infantry (City of Glasgow Regiment)

Seaforth Highlanders (Ross-shire Buffs, The Duke of Albany's)
   The Officers wore a badge similar to that of the other ranks, but with
   the cypher 'L' and a coronet between the antlers.

The Gordon Highlanders

The Queen's Own Cameron Highlanders—blue hackle

The Royal Ulster Rifles—pipers wear a black hackle

The Royal Irish Fusiliers (Princess Victoria's)—green hackle

The Argyll and Sutherland Highlanders (Princess Louise's)

The Rifle Brigade (Prince Consort's Own)

The Lowland Regiment

The Highland Regiment

Formation Signs (*Pl. 13–14*)

Plate 13. Infantry Divisions

The formation sign of the 1st Division was a white equilateral triangle, on
its own or on a black, square background. The triangle represented the
top of the spearhead badge of 1st Corps as this was the first division of the
B.E.F. in France. Subsequently, the 1st Division landed in North Africa
with the 1st Army, and later took part in the Italian campaign.

   The badge of the 2nd Division was chosen in 1940 by its commander,
Major-General H. C. Lloyd, who had previously commanded a Guards
Brigade with a single key as its sign. The crossed keys were the emblem

of the Archbishop of York and used to be carried on the shields and banners of his army. This was also the badge of the 5th Infantry Brigade. The Division fought in France with the B.E.F. and later in the Far East.

The 3rd Division was also in France with the B.E.F. and later with the 21st Army Group.

The 4th Division was sent to France in October, 1939, later taking part in the operations in North Africa, Italy and Greece. Initially its badge was the fourth quadrant of a circle, but later became a circle with the fourth quadrant detached, as illustrated.

The 5th was a Yorkshire division. It served with the B.E.F. and later one of its brigades was sent to Norway. Afterwards the division was sent to Madagascar, and from there to India and Iraq. It was later employed in Italy and finally in north-western Europe.

The 6th Division served with the B.E.F., in the Western Desert, in Syria, and later in Tobruk during the siege, where it was renumbered the 70th and, as such, was sent to India.

The 9th (Scottish) Division was raised in 1939 and amalgamated in 1940 with the 51st Division, the latter having been depleted in France.

The 12th Division took part in the first stage of the war in France and was subsequently disbanded.

The 13th Division re-adopted the sign it had worn during World War 1. It was reformed in Greece in the winter of 1945–46 during the campaign against E.L.A.S., drafting the British units of the 4th Indian Division due to return to India. The sign was chosen as an omen of good luck; the horse-shoe was intended to combat the unlucky number 13.

The 15th (Scottish) Division saw service in north-western Europe.

The formation sign of the 18th Division represents a windmill, in association with East Anglia where it was raised. It was sent to Singapore just before the Japanese invasion.

The rose of the 23rd Division could be found on a blue or green background. This division took part in the first campaign in France and later, back in Britain, was disbanded.

The 36th Division fought against the Japanese. The emblem of its 29th Brigade and that of its 72nd were linked together to form the divisional sign.

The 38th (Welsh) Division carried the yellow cross of St. David in its sign as it was a second-line division made up of Welsh Territorial units. It remained in the Home Forces for the duration of the war.

The 40th Division was formed in Sicily in 1943. The World War 1 sign portrayed a bantam cock, but to commemorate the battle of Bourlon Wood an acorn and an oak leaf on a white diamond was superimposed. In World War 2 only the acorn remained as the sign.

The 42nd (East Lancashire) Division's badge has not been illustrated in this plate because, as early as 1941, it was converted into an armoured division and is included on Plate 4.

The 43rd (Wessex) Division adopted as its badge the arms of the kings of Wessex. It was a division of the 21st Army Group.

The 44th (Home Counties) Division saw active service in France and was then sent to the Middle East. It was disbanded after the battle of El Alamein where it fought in the Southern sector of the front line.

The 45th (Wessex) Division was a second-line territorial division and as such was part of the Home Forces. Its formation sign was Drake's drum.

The 46th (North Midlands) Division served with the B.E.F. and later with the 1st Army in Tunisia. It took part in the Italian campaign and saw a spell of service in Greece.

The 47th (London) Division adopted the 'Bow Bells' as its badge and was part of the Home Forces.

The 48th (South Midlands) Division, like the 47th, did not serve abroad. The badge shows a macaw as, when its commander first entered the divisional headquarters at Littlecote, a macaw kept in the house shouted 'Good luck, good luck!'

The 49th (West Riding) Division initially wore its World War 1 badge, the white rose of York. It was sent to Norway in 1940, and then to Iceland where it adopted the familiar 'polar bear' sign. At first the bear had a bowed head, but this was later raised to make it appear more aggressive. Back in Britain, in 1943, the division joined the 21st Army Group then training for the invasion of Europe.

The double 'T' badge of the 50th (Northumbrian) Division could be seen until a couple of years ago on a large H.Q. sign at Kirklevington, Teesside. The division took part in operations with the B.E.F. and later with the 8th Army in North Africa. It took part in the invasion of north-western Europe and in the liberation of Norway.

The 51st (Highland) Division fought some pitched battles in France and after the Dunkirk evacuation was moved to the Middle East. After the conquest of North Africa and Sicily it was repatriated in time to join the 21st Army Group.

The formation sign of the 52nd (Lowland) Division was St. Andrew's cross on a shield and, as it had been trained for mountain warfare, had the word 'Mountain' on a scroll below the shield. It was in France with the B.E.F. and returned to the continent as part of the 21st Army Group.

The 53rd (Welsh) Division landed in Normandy and subsequently took part in the invasion of north-western Europe.

The 54th (East Anglian) Division adopted the initials of the name of its commander, Major-General J. H. T. Priestman, as its badge. It was drafted into the 'Line of Communications' of the 21st Army Group, its 162nd Independent Brigade still wearing the 'JP' sign.

The 55th (West Lancashire) Division stayed in Britain engaged in a training role. Its badge depicts the red rose of Lancaster with its double set of 5 leaves representing the double 5.

The 56th (London) Division adopted Dick Whittington's cat as its badge. It was posted in the area of Palestine–Syria–Iraq as a security force. Later it took an active part in the Italian campaign.

The 59th Division was part of the 21st Army Group. Pithead machinery against a slag heap was its badge.

The 61st, 76th, 77th and 80th Divisions did not serve overseas, but were employed in a training role as part of the Home Forces.

The 78th Division was part of the 1st Army in North Africa; later taking part in the Italian campaign, it reached Austria in May, 1945.

Plate 14. Independent Infantry Brigades and Brigade Groups

The 1st and 24th Independent Guards Brigade Groups, the 32nd Independent Guards Brigade and the 33rd Guards Brigade all wore formation signs in the colours of the Household Brigade: blue and red. The same colours were also used in the signs of brigades which were converted from artillery units; the 301st and 304th Infantry Brigades' signs even displayed artillery emblems, i.e. the crossed guns and crossed searchlight beams.

The design and colour of some formation signs were borrowed from the traditions of the brigade's battalions, i.e. the Irish shamrock of the 38th Infantry Brigade, the sphinx of the 56th, and the colours in the formation signs of the 70th, 71st, 204th, etc. Independent Infantry Brigades.

Regional associations were shown, e.g. the arms of Cornwall in the sign of the 73rd Independent Infantry Brigade, previously worn by personnel of the Devon and Cornwall County Division. The tulip of the 212th Independent Infantry Brigade was previously worn by the Lincolnshire County Division, and the seaxes of the 223rd marked the Brigade's association with Essex.

The King chessman was the emblem of the 206th Independent Infantry Brigade. The 1st Battalion Dorsetshire Regiment, the 1st Battalion Hampshire Regiment and the 2nd Battalion Devonshire Regiment were brigaded together during the defence of Malta, and adopted the Maltese cross as their brigade's badge.

The 29th and 31st were Independent Brigade Groups.

The Airborne Forces (*Pl. 15*)

The first British parachute units were born in June, 1940, on the personal instruction of the Prime Minister, Mr. Winston Churchill. As the Commandos were being raised at the same time, No. 2 Commando underwent parachute training. In November, 1940, it became the 11th Special Air Service Battalion, divided into two wings: Parachute Wing and Glider Wing.

The first war action carried out by parachutists was inspired by the commandos. On the night of 10 February, 1941, 'X' Troop of the 11th S.A.S. Battalion landed in the south of Italy and succeeded in blowing up the aqueduct of Tragino.

In September, 1941, the 11th S.A.S. Battalion became the 1st Parachute Battalion, the first of four battalions of the 1st Parachute Brigade.

The 4th Battalion later participated in the formation of the 2nd Parachute Brigade, together with the 5th (Scottish) Battalion and 6th (Welsh) Battalion.

Three battalions were raised in India: the 151st, later transferred to the Middle East and renumbered 156th, the 152nd Indian and 153rd Gurkha Parachute Battalions. The 10th Parachute Battalion was raised in Palestine, and the 11th was formed by a nucleus of parachutists of the 156th.

Thus the 10th, the 11th and the 156th Parachute Battalions formed the 4th Parachute Brigade. The 1st, 2nd and 4th Parachute Brigades and the 1st Air Landing Brigade, by June, 1943, had formed the 1st Airborne Division.

While the 1st Airborne Division was taking part in the North African campaign of General Eisenhower, and later in the Italian campaign, the 6th Airborne Division was being raised in Britain. Eventually it was composed of the 3rd Parachute Brigade, which in its turn was composed of the Canadian Parachute Battalion and the 8th (Midland Counties) and 9th (Home Counties) Battalions.

The 5th Parachute Brigade was formed of the 7th (Light Infantry), 12th (Yorkshire) and 13th (Lancashire) Battalions.

The 6th Air Landing Brigade was composed of the Glider Pilot Regiment and the Airborne Infantry Battalions it carried.

In November, 1943, the 1st Airborne Division (minus the 2nd Brigade) came to Britain to join the Allied Airborne Army in training for the invasion of Europe. The 6th Airborne Division took part in the Normandy landing and the 1st Division later joined in the campaign at Arnhem.

Meanwhile the 2nd Independent Parachute Brigade saw active service in Italy and Greece and took part in operation 'Anvil', the invasion of southern France.

The Army Commandos (*pl. 15 and 16*)

The first Commandos were formed in June 1940, each consisting of five troops, with fifty men to each troop. Later, in 1941, they were reorganised into six troops of sixty-five.

Only three weeks after the idea of raising such a force had been conceived, the first raid on the French coast took place during the night of 23–24 June. Many others followed.

In February, 1941, Nos. 7, 8 and 11 Commandos were sent to the Middle East to join forces with Nos. 50–52, who amalgamated to form the Combined (Middle East) Commando. Nos. 7, 8 and 11 formed respectively 'A', 'B' and 'C' Battalions and the Combined (Middle East) Commando became 'D' Battalion of 'Layforce', a brigade of the 8th Army's 6th Division. The brigade was named after its commander, Lieutenant-Colonel R. E. Laycock, later to become Chief of Combined Operations. After fighting in North Africa, Syria and Crete, Layforce was disbanded and Laycock returned to Britain to command the Special Service Brigade.

Subsequently, four Special Service Brigades were formed grouping together the Army and the Royal Marine Commandos. The first two of the R.M. Commandos, Nos. 40 and 41, were raised in October, 1942.

The Special Service Group was made up of the 1st Special Service Brigade (Nos. 3, 4 and 6 Commandos, 45 R.M. Commando and 1st and 8th Troops of the No. 10 (Inter-Allied) Commando) and by the 4th Special Service Brigade composed of R.M. Commandos. It took part in the invasion of north-western Europe.

The 2nd Special Service Brigade was in Italy, composed of Nos. 2 and 3 Commandos, and Nos. 40 and 41 R.M. Commandos. The 3rd Special Service Brigade formed by Nos. 1 and 5 Commandos and Nos. 42 and 44 R.M. Commandos served in the Far East.

Nos. 1 and 6 Commandos took part in the landings in French North Africa, and were used in an infantry role during the following winter campaign.

No. 10 (Inter-Allied) Commando was formed of French, Belgian, Dutch, Norwegian and Polish troops, the 10th ('X') Troop mainly made up of Germans and Austrians. This Commando was then broken up and its troops used in different raids and on different fronts.

Towards the end of 1944 the Special Service Brigades were renamed Commando Brigades.

Plate 15. The Airborne Forces

The Pegasus badge was worn by members of both 1st and 6th Airborne Divisions. The first parachute units adopted the PARACHUTE shoulder title, also with the '1', '2' and '3' battalion figures incorporated below. It should be mentioned that the 1st Parachute Battalion wore a green lanyard, the 2nd a yellow lanyard, the 3rd a red and the 4th a black lanyard. For the duration of the war the 4th painted its equipment black.

The 5th was a Scottish battalion and wore the Balmoral bonnet, with an Army Air Corps badge on a Hunting Stuart tartan patch, until September, 1944. The 6th Parachute Battalion was of Welsh extraction, and its members wore the Welsh black flash at the back of the collar.

The 12th Battalion wore a light blue lanyard.

The Parachute Regiment came into being in 1942 and, together with the Glider Pilot Regiment, adopted appropriate shoulder titles, dark blue lettering on a pale blue background.

The red beret was first worn by the regiment when it went to North Africa in November, 1942.

The 21st and 22nd Independent Parachute Companies were the 'pathfinder' units, respectively belonging to the 1st and 6th Airborne Divisions.

Special Forces Cap Badges

The common feature of the commandos' uniform was the green beret. The commandos raised in the Middle East adopted a 'knuckle-duster' knife as their cap badge and, initially, No. 2 Commando wore a dagger in between two letters 'S', for Special Service. No. 6 Commando wore a roman VI embroidered on a square black patch, and No. 9 Commando a black hackle.

The first recruits of the Special Air Service came from Layforce and initially they operated in the Western Desert in conjunction with the Long Range Desert Group. Later S.A.S. became operationally independent and split into the Special Raiding Squadron and the Special Boat Service; the latter specialised in amphibious warfare in the Aegean.

In time the 1st and 2nd Special Air Service Regiments came into being, and in March, 1944, together with two French parachute battalions and a Belgian parachute company, they formed the Special Air Service Brigade, that was used in north-west Europe before and after D Day.

The Raiding Support Regiment was raised in 1943 and served on both sides of the Adriatic before disbandment in 1945. Like that of the S.A.S., its cap badge was embroidered in coloured thread.

The Long Range Desert Group and Popski's Private Army were units for raiding and reconnaissance operations. Both raised in the Middle East, they followed the 8th Army and were disbanded in 1945. The former wore brass, bronze and white metal cap badges. The cap badges of the P.P.A. were generally made in brass, but some white metal and silver badges were made in Italy.

'V' Force was formed of British servicemen and Indians, many belonging to the hill tribes of Burma, and was employed behind the Japanese lines.

Wings

Glider Pilot and S.A.S. wings were worn on the left breast, above the medal ribbons or above the pocket; all qualified parachutists of the Regular Army wore their badges on the upper right sleeve, below the shoulder title.

Parachutists and Glider Pilots, other than Regular Army, wore a white parachute or a glider embroidered in pale blue on the forearm of the left sleeve.

Plate 16. Commando Shoulder Flashes

The formation sign of Combined Operations symbolically depicted its role and was red on black. Early in 1944 all commando units began to wear the red dagger on a triangular black background.

A number of shoulder flashes have been worn by different units in different periods, and only some are illustrated. Some troops wore a special badge: for instance, the 101st Troop of No. 6 Commando. 'V' Force's badge could be found embroidered on dark green felt or woven on khaki. The Special Boat Service badge was made in metal and enamel.

However, during the war, all units were issued with printed shoulder titles, such as that of No. 6 Commando (illustrated). The set covered No. 1 to No. 12 Commando, plus F.F. (Free French) Commando and Commando S.B.S.

Poland

Poland became a unified nation in the 10th century and, because of its position in the heart of Europe, it fought a succession of wars against the neighbouring states, until, in 1772, its first partition took place.

Another partition of Poland took place in 1793 and yet another two years later. Soon after, the Polish lancers of the Napoleonic Army became well known on the battlefields of Europe. Their headdress was a tall, flat-topped, square-shaped 'czapka' with a spreadeagle clutching an 'Amazon' shield at the front.

Napoleon formed the Duchy of Warsaw, but after his defeat in 1813 the Duchy ceased to exist and Poland once again came under the control of its powerful neighbours: Austria, Prussia and Russia.

The outbreak of World War 1 found the Poles politically divided, although the aim of all parties was to achieve Polish national independence.

Polish units were raised by either contendant and finally, in November, 1918, Poland achieved its independence.

The Polish Army was initially formed from various units which came back to Poland after the war still wearing different uniforms, predominantly Austrian, German and French, although Russian and even Italian uniforms were in use at the time.

The first 'dress' regulations and Polish uniforms appeared in 1919.

Later, in the 1930s, new regulations were issued which gradually changed the uniforms until, in 1939, all the officers wore:

The evening dress, that consisted of a khaki tunic (model 1936) and dark trousers with double lateral stripes and piping within. A special silk evening belt was also worn with this uniform.

The garrison or walking-out uniform, made of khaki material, and consisting of tunic (model 1936) and breeches or long trousers.

The field uniform, exactly the same as the above, but without any patches and badges, except rank insignia that were still present on the shoulder straps. For summer the tunic was made of a light khaki dress linen.

The non-commissioned officers were entitled to the same uniforms. A notable difference was that they had only single stripes on the evening trousers, instead of the double stripes and piping worn by officers.

The other ranks were issued with two basic uniforms: a 'walking-out' dress and the field service uniform, both introduced in 1936. The 1919 tunic, without breast pockets, was no longer manufactured after 1936, although it was still worn by a few regiments during World War 2.

The pattern of the greatcoat was identical for officers and men alike, the only difference being in the quality of the cloth. Officers and senior N.C.O.s also wore ankle-length capes without buttons. All ranks serving in the mountain divisions were also issued with capes, but theirs were shorter and with six buttons. A black leather coat could also be worn by personnel of the tank battalions and motorised units.

The outstanding features of the Polish uniform have always been the square-shaped, peaked cap ('czapka') and the 'zigzag' ornament worn by all ranks on the collar of the tunic.

It should be added that officers and warrant officers wore the 'czapka' with a metal rim around the visor; all ranks of the three Light Horse regiments and of the Frontier Defence Corps wore instead a normal, round-peaked cap with metal-rimmed visor.

All ranks of the 21st and 22nd Mountain Divisions wore a stiff felt 'dress' hat with the Polish eagle and rank badges at the front, and a feather on a cluster of downy feathers was attached onto the side of this hat. The feathers were also worn on the 'czapka'.

Another mountain division, the 11th, was formed before the war but only its band and the 1st Battalion of the 49th Regiment were issued with special hats. The hat of the 11th (Carpathian) Mountain Division was modelled on the hats used by the southern Carpathian mountaineers, called 'Huculi'.

The forage cap was the standard field cap until 1937 when a new headdress was introduced: it was a square-topped cap with a soft peak and folding sides that could be lowered to cover the ears. However, in 1939, both headdresses were still worn as the forage cap remained very popular, particularly among the cavalry, some units of which also wore a regimental collar pennon on its left side.

Personnel of armoured, motorised and anti-aircraft units wore black berets.

Just before the outbreak of World War 2, a new Polish steel helmet started to be issued to the infantry, while the remainder of the Army wore helmets of French pattern.

The colour of the band of the peaked cap and the colour of the stripes on the evening dress trousers showed corps, service or regimental distinctions.

The evening dress trousers were khaki for generals and officers of the Ordnance, Administrative and Geographical Services and Commissariat. All officers of the Artillery (except Horse Artillery), Engineers and Signals wore dark green trousers. The Infantry, Cavalry, Horse Artillery and all the other corps and services not mentioned above wore dark blue evening trousers.

The officers' trousers had broad double stripes with piping in between;

the regular N.C.O.s wore a single stripe, 40 mm wide, instead.

A list of cap bands and evening trousers' stripes colours is given below:

	Cap Band	*Stripes/Piping*
Generals	khaki	dark blue/dark blue
Infantry-Highland Rifles	dark blue	yellow/yellow
Rifle Battalions	dark blue	yellow/yellow
1st Light Horse	crimson	crimson/white
2nd Light Horse	white	white/white
3rd Light Horse	yellow	yellow/yellow
1st Lancers	crimson	crimson/crimson
2nd Lancers	white	white/white
3rd Lancers	yellow	yellow/yellow
4th Lancers	cornflower blue	cornflower blue/ cornflower blue
5th Lancers	cherry red	cherry red/cherry red
6th Lancers	light blue	light blue/light blue
7th Lancers	crimson	crimson/white
8th Lancers	dark yellow	dark yellow/dark yellow
9th Lancers	crimson	crimson/white
10th Lancers	crimson	crimson/crimson
11th Lancers	white	white/white
12th Lancers	crimson	crimson/crimson
13th Lancers	pink	pink/pink
14th Lancers	yellow	yellow/yellow
15th Lancers	scarlet	scarlet/scarlet
16th Lancers	white	white/white
17th Lancers	yellow	yellow/yellow
18th Lancers	cornflower blue	cornflower blue/ cornflower blue
19th Lancers	dark blue	white/white
20th Lancers	crimson	crimson/crimson
21st Lancers	turquoise	turquoise/turquoise
22nd Lancers	white	white/white
23rd Lancers	orange	orange/orange
24th Lancers	white	white/white
25th Lancers	scarlet	scarlet/scarlet
26th Lancers	pink	pink/pink
27th Lancers	yellow	yellow/yellow
1st Mounted Rifles	crimson	crimson/crimson
2nd Mounted Rifles	crimson	crimson/crimson
3rd Mounted Rifles	crimson	crimson/crimson

	Cap Band	*Stripes/Piping*
4th Mounted Rifles	crimson	crimson/crimson
5th Mounted Rifles	white	white/white
6th Mounted Rifles	white	white/white
7th Mounted Rifles	white	white/white
8th Mounted Rifles	white	white/white
9th Mounted Rifles	yellow	yellow/yellow
10th Mounted Rifles	yellow	yellow/yellow
Mounted Pioneers	scarlet	scarlet/scarlet
Recce (Mot. Bde)	crimson	crimson/green
Anti-Tank (Mot. Bde)	scarlet	scarlet/orange
Field Artillery	*dark green	scarlet/scarlet
Medium Artillery	*dark green	scarlet/scarlet
Heavy Artillery	*dark green	scarlet/scarlet
Motorised Artillery	dark green	scarlet/scarlet
Horse Artillery	*black	scarlet/scarlet
Anti-Aircraft Artillery	*dark green	scarlet/scarlet
Survey Artillery	*dark green	scarlet/scarlet
Armoured Corps	orange	orange/orange
Engineers	*black	raspberry red/raspberry red
Signals	*black	cornflower blue/cornflower blue
Train	sky blue	sky blue/crimson
Military Police	scarlet	scarlet/yellow
Ordnance	khaki	none
Admin./Supply	khaki	none
Medical Service	*cherry red	cherry red/sky blue
Legal Service	khaki	none
Geographical Service	khaki	none
Commissaries	khaki	none

* Denotes velvet

Plate 17. Officers' Rank Badges

All ranks of the Polish Army wore the same cap badge on the upper front of the headdress: the cap badge depicting the Polish eagle holding an 'Amazon' shield, was made in white metal or oxidised silver.

A small version of this badge was worn on the forage cap, and a small embroidered badge was worn on the field cap.

The generals wore a large silver-embroidered 'zigzag' ornament on the band of the peaked cap together with a stripe of silver braid and rank stars, the latter at the front under the cap badge.

All the other officers also wore rank stars on the cap band; the senior officers with two stripes of silver braid, the others with one stripe only.

Two stripes of silver braid were carried from corner to corner across the top of the 'czapka' and down the sides, ending under the cap band. The generals wore a khaki cap band while most officers wore the coloured bands which have been described in the previous pages.

Generals had the 'zigzag' ornament embroidered on the outside edges of the collar patches, on the shoulder straps, and also on the cuffs of the tunic. The officers' 'zigzag' was narrower than that of the generals and was the same for senior and junior officers, worn on the collar only.

Marshals wore a silver eagle clutching crossed batons on the collar patches (Plate 18) and on the shoulder straps they had the crossed batons only, embroidered above the 'zigzag' device.

All the generals had a silver embroidered eagle on the collar patches and stars on the shoulder straps.

The same eagle, but in silver metal, was worn on the collar by officers of the General Staff (Plate 18).

Plate 18. Officers' Rank Badges

The basic rank badge of Polish officers and generals alike was the five-pointed star, embroidered in silver wire on the shoulder straps. The senior officers were distinguished by 5-mm double bars embroidered in silver wire on the shoulder straps, at 15 mm from the seam. Regimental numbers and monograms were usually embroidered at 7·5 mm from the seam and, in the case of senior officers, they were evenly embroidered across the double bars.

Monograms for Cavalry Shoulder Straps

The monograms worn on the shoulder straps were usually 30 mm high, made in silver wire embroidery for officers and warrant officers, and in white metal for the other ranks. They were the monograms of illustrious Polish generals and leaders, some of them at one time connected with the regiment; those illustrated in Plate 18 were mostly adopted in the 1930s by regiments of Light Horse, Lancers and Mounted Rifles.

A list of all the cavalry regiments, with number and full regimental title, is given further on in these pages and should be consulted in order to decipher the meaning of the monograms.

Plate 19. Warrant Officers' and N.C.O.s' Rank Badges

The warrant officer of the Polish Army wore one silver star at the front of the cap and on the shoulder straps. He also wore stripes on the 'czapka', as did the officers, but in dark red instead of silver.

The staff-sergeant and sergeant wore chevrons on the cap and on the shoulder straps; the other ranks wore stripes instead.

Chevrons and stripes were embroidered in silver on red felt when used on the cap, and they were made of braid on the shoulder straps. The chevrons were set at a 90° angle. The arms of those on the cap were 25 mm long and the stripes 25 × 4 mm in size.

The warrant officers wore the same 'zigzag' on the collar as officers, while the other N.C.O.s wore a simpler pattern of the same device, embroidered in silver. The 'zigzag' of the soldiers was made of silver braid.

There were two types of braid for use on the shoulder straps. The first was a silver braid with narrow red stripes on the edges that was used by warrant officers and non-commissioned officers of the Army and by cadets of the Reserve. The shoulder straps of the latter had an additional edging made of two twisted cords: one red and one white. The silver and red symbolise the white and red of the Polish national flag.

The cadets of the Regular Army wore different shoulder straps altogether. They had silver piping and all-silver braid and the monogram 'SP' (Szkoła Podchorążych), and their shoulder straps were made of coloured cloth, with coloured piping showing between the silver piping and the silver braid.

The colours of the Regular Army cadets' shoulder straps were:

	Shoulder Strap	Piping
Infantry	yellow	dark blue
Cavalry	crimson	dark blue
Artillery	green	black
Anti-Aircraft Artillery	green	yellow
Engineers	black	scarlet
Signals	black	cornflower blue
Armoured Corps	orange	black
Medical Service	cherry red	dark blue

Cadets were trained in different army colleges. Medical cadets attended additional lectures at Warsaw University and engineer cadets at Warsaw Polytechnic. The training lasted three years with the exception of the medical and engineering training which lasted on average six and four years respectively.

A Regular Army cadet wore a narrow silver braid stripe around the top and along the seam of the cuff for each year of college training. During the fourth year he wore a thick stripe representing the first three years and a narrow stripe for the additional year. Another narrow stripe was added for each successive year of training.

The training of reserve officers was carried out in Cadet Officers'

Schools and, on completion of the courses, they wore a stripe of red-edged silver braid around the top of the cuffs, but not down the seam.

All cadets were given N.C.O. ranks and wore special white metal badges on the collar, as illustrated, above their corresponding shoulder straps.

Plate 20. Collar Patches

Collar patches were worn on the collar of the tunic, with the 'zigzag' ornament embroidered or stitched along the front and bottom sides. They were usually made in felt, although officers of certain corps and services had velvet collar patches.

A complete set of collar patches has been illustrated as they were worn on the tunic adopted in 1936, and the officers' collar patches, made in velvet (both patch and piping), have been marked * in the following list.

	Collar Patch	Piping
Generals	dark blue	crimson
Infantry	dark blue	yellow
Infantry (Frontier Defence Corps)	dark blue	dark green
Rifle Battalions	dark blue	nile green
Field Artillery	*dark green	black
Medium Artillery	*dark green	scarlet
Heavy Artillery	*dark green	crimson
Survey Artillery	*dark green	white
Anti-Aircraft Artillery	*dark green	yellow
Engineers	*black	scarlet
Railway Engineers	*black	crimson
Ordnance	emerald green	black
Signals	*black	cornflower blue
Military Police	scarlet	light yellow
Legal Service	*raspberry red	black
Geographical Service	*black	white
Commissaries	black	scarlet
Administrative Service	royal blue	cherry red
Chaplains	*violet	none
Medical Service—Doctors	*cherry red	dark blue
Pharmacists	*cherry red	cornflower blue
Dentists	*cherry red	light blue
Veterinaries	*cherry red	dark green

Collar patches were worn on the greatcoat collar, in the form of two 5-mm stripes, except by those units which wore pennons. The colour of the patch was represented by the stripe at the bottom, the stripe at the top represented the piping of the normal collar patch.

All Mounted troops wore 'pennons' on the collar of the tunic and great-coat instead of collar patches, and they were miniature replicas of the pennons worn on the cavalry lances.

The 'zigzag' ornament, in this case, was embroidered directly onto the collar of the tunic and the pennon was sewn above it. With the adoption of the 1936 tunic with pointed collar, the pennons also took on a pointed shape.

The correct way to show these badges graphically remains, however, the rectangular shape worn before 1936.

The colours of the Polish cavalry were crimson and dark blue; Horse Artillery wore black and scarlet pennons, and Mounted Pioneers the same colours reversed. The cavalry squadrons of the Frontier Defence Corps had dark blue and dark green pennons, the signal squadrons black and cornflower blue. Light blue with a crimson stripe were the pennon colours of the supply train.

The Armoured units wore a triangular pennon half black and half orange on the tunic's collar and greatcoat collar. The orange, together with crimson and green, were adopted as the colours of the bi-pointed pennons of the Reconnaissance units, and the pennons of the Anti-Tank units of the motorised brigade were in red and black.

Plate 21. Collar Patches

All three regiments of Light Horse wore silver collar pennons, the first two with a crimson stripe in the centre, the 3rd with a yellow stripe. The regiments could be further distinguished one from the other by the differently coloured stripes on the evening dress trousers and cap bands.

The colours of the Lancers' pennons were as follows:

1st Lancers	crimson–white
2nd Lancers	white–dark blue
3rd Lancers	yellow–white
4th Lancers	cornflower blue–white
5th Lancers	cherry red–white–cornflower blue
6th Lancers	light blue–white–light blue
7th Lancers	crimson–white–crimson
8th Lancers	dark yellow
9th Lancers	crimson–white–crimson–white
10th Lancers	crimson–white–dark blue–white
11th Lancers	crimson–white–crimson
12th Lancers	crimson–white–dark blue
13th Lancers	pink–cornflower blue–pink
14th Lancers	yellow–white–yellow
15th Lancers	white–scarlet

16th Lancers	dark blue–scarlet–white
17th Lancers	white–scarlet–yellow
18th Lancers	white–scarlet–cornflower blue
19th Lancers	dark blue–white–dark blue
20th Lancers	crimson–dark blue–white–crimson
21st Lancers	turquoise–yellow–white–turquoise
22nd Lancers	white–crimson–white
23rd Lancers	orange–white–orange–white
24th Lancers	white–yellow–white
25th Lancers	white–cornflower blue–scarlet
26th Lancers	pink–cornflower blue–white
27th Lancers	yellow–white–dark blue–white

The basic colour of the Mounted Rifles was dark green and this was combined with other colours to form the pennons of the Mounted Rifles regiments. They were:

1st Mounted Rifles	dark green–crimson
2nd Mounted Rifles	dark green–blue–crimson
3rd Mounted Rifles	dark green–yellow–crimson
4th Mounted Rifles	dark green–white–crimson
5th Mounted Rifles	dakk green–crimson–white
6th Mounted Rifles	dark green–white
7th Mounted Rifles	dark green–yellow–white
8th Mounted Rifles	dark green–blue–white
9th Mounted Rifles	dark green–crimson–yellow
10th Mounted Rifles	dark green–white–yellow

Plate 22. Collar Badges

Metal badges were worn on the collar to indicate a particular branch of service, or as a regimental distinction.

Officers of the General Staff wore an eagle similar to that of generals, but in silver metal instead of silver embroidery. The reason for this difference was that the eagle of the generals represented a permanent rank while that of the staff officers represented an appointment only and, therefore the metal badge could be taken off when necessary.

The Naval Service badge was used by Army officers on duty with the Navy in harbours, coastal defence, etc.

The 48th, 49th and 53rd Infantry Regiments, together with all other units of the 11th (Carpathian) Mountain Division, wore the double cross on mountain pine twigs and oak leaves as collar badge and feather holder. Regiments of the 21st and 22nd Mountain Divisions (from 1st to 6th Highland (Podhale) Regiments, 21st and 22nd Field Artillery and other divisional units) wore the swastika on pine twigs. This design was changed just before World War 2, the swastika being turned anti-clockwise.

There were three branches of Christian chaplains in the Polish Army: Catholic, Protestant and Orthodox, each wearing a different cross (illustrated from left to right on this plate). Rabbis wore plain violet collar patches.

Craftsmen and personnel of N.C.O. schools wore their own badges and bandsmen wore a lyre; the bandmasters wore a lyre over two oak leaves.

The 1st (Tartar) Squadron of the 13th Lancers had collar badges pinned on the collar pennons in pairs with the stars facing inwards.

The 44th Infantry Regiment traces its origin to a World War 1 rifle legion of Polish-American volunteers and wore white metal bugles (22 × 17 mm) on the collar, with the mouthpieces facing inward.

The Headquarters of the 16th Infantry Division (and the 16th Field Artillery Regiment of the same division) wore enamelled collar badges (21 × 25 mm) and differently-designed enamelled badges were also adopted by each of the divisional infantry regiments 64th, 65th and 66th.

The other pairs of collar badges were worn all facing one way; for instance, the lion of the 40th and the mounted knight of the 85th Regiment.

On the collar of the greatcoat, the badges were positioned below the coloured stripes.

Plate 23. Monograms and Badges for Shoulder Straps

The monograms were usually embroidered in silver wire on officers' and warrant officers' shoulder straps and in white metal for the other ranks.

N.C.O.s could also wear embroidered badges on uniforms they had purchased privately.

The badge of the Presidential Guard was initially the letters 'O' and 'Z' interlaced (Oddział Zamkowy), but later a Polish eagle (30 mm tall) was adopted instead.

The 1st, 5th, 6th, 41st and 66th Infantry Regiments wore the initials of Joseph Piłsudski (also worn by the 1st Light Horse) and, when the famous Marshal died in 1935, they adopted black piping around the left shoulder strap.

The 37th Infantry Regiment and the 8th Lancers were named after Prince Joseph Poniatowski, Commander-in-Chief of the army of the Grand Duchy of Warsaw and Marshal of the French Empire.

The list of regiments of the Polish Army (p. 137) will help to clarify the meaning of the monograms.

The bear of the 77th Infantry Regiment was the emblem of Samogatia, the medieval name of part of East Prussia–Lithuania.

All ranks of the Marine Rifle Battalion wore an anchor on the shoulder straps. The Battalion was part of the Army and was detailed for coastal defence.

Engineers wore initials related to their specialisation on the shoulder straps: 'R' was the initial used by the Radiotelegraphic Regiment. An 'M' was worn by the Bridging (Mostowy) Engineers; an 'E' by the Electro-technical Engineers and an 'S' was worn by Engineers attached to the narrow-gauge railways.

The other units wore regimental numbers, embroidered in silver wire for officers and warrant officers, in white metal for the other ranks.

Commemorative Badges

Special badges were worn by regiments and other formations of the Polish Army, and by colleges and training centres. These were not strictly in-tended for identification purposes, but were generally awarded on fulfil-ment of certain conditions, i.e. for serving in the unit for one year during a war, or after three months service at the front. In peacetime they were awarded after one year of active service, or, in the case of the Reserve, for having participated in two army manoeuvres. The badge was generally awarded on the regimental day, or on completion of manoeuvres, and could be withdrawn from deserters or as some other disciplinary punish-ment.

They were worn on the left breast pocket, 4 cm below the button, only the Staff College badge was worn on the right breast pocket and the badges of the Armoured Corps and Signals were worn above the ribbons. The badges were normally made in enamel for officers and warrant officers and plain metal for the other ranks, but some regiments had the same badge for all ranks. Both types have been illustrated together in this volume.

Some regiments had names taken from geographical locations with which they were historically associated. Some took the name of the most important among their battle honours or they were named after honorary 'chiefs', i.e. former Polish kings, national heroes and famous soldiers and, in certain cases, the regiment was named after late com-manding officers or living generals. For instance, 3 Pułk Szwoleżerów Mazowieckich Imenia Pułkownika Jana Kozietulskiego can be translated as: 3rd Regiment of Light Horse of the region of Mazovia, named after Colonel Jan Kozietulski, who led the charge of the Polish Light Horse (Chevau-Lègers) of the Imperial Guard at Somo Sierra in 1807.

A list of regiments as they existed in 1939, with full regimental titles, is given on pages 137–40, together with some information relating to the badges they wore.

Infantry Regimental Badges (*Pl. 24, 25, 26*)

Blue and yellow were the predominant colours of the infantry badges, although other colours were used as well.

Regiments with the word 'Legion' in their title were those raised from the Volunteer Polish Legions of World War 1. The centre pieces of the badges of the 1st, 5th and 6th Infantry Regiments were actually replicas of that of the 1st Brigade of Legions. The centre piece of the badge of the 2nd Regiment was a replica of that of the 2nd Brigade and also the badges of the 3rd and 4th Regiments incorporated motifs of World War 1 badges.

The 14th Infantry was a regiment from the region of Kujawy and the 15th was known as the wolves' regiment and thus had four wolves' heads in its badge. The mermaid with sword was taken from the coat of arms of Warsaw and can be seen in the badges of the 19th and 21st Regiments: the 19th was named after the 'Relief of Lwów'; the 21st after the city of Warsaw.

A monument built in honour of T. Kościuszko and the walls of Kraków are shown in the badge of the 20th and the soldier in the badge of the 23rd is Colonel L. Lis-Kula, to whom the regiment was dedicated.

The ribbon of the *Virtuti Militari* Order and the decoration itself can be seen respectively in the badges of the 22nd and 56th.

The Cross of Kaniów, with an eagle on crossed swords, is depicted in the badges of the 29th, 30th and 31st Infantry Regiments. The four emblems in the badge of the 36th are those of Warsaw University, Warsaw Polytechnic, the Central Agricultural College and the Central College of Commerce. The regiment was called 'Academy Legion'.

The coat of arms of Savoy, or the Italian colours, are part of the badges of the 42nd, 50th, 51st, 52nd and 81st Regiments and the white Cross of Savoy is depicted in the badge of the 53rd. Francesco Nullo, to whom the 50th Regiment was dedicated, was an Italian patriot who fought in Poland during the 1863 revolution.

The words 'Dzieci Lwowskie' which appear in the regimental title of the 40th mean 'Children of Lwów'. The 81st Regiment was raised in Grodno and dedicated to King Stefan Batory.

French emblems or colours were incorporated in the badges of the 42nd, 43rd (Bayonne Legion), 49th and 52nd, the latter a rifle regiment from the eastern region of the Kresy.

The badge of the 58th portrayed King Bolesław Chrobry, the founder of Gniezno, where the regiment was raised. The coat of arms of this town is shown among others in the badge of the 69th.

The badges of the 59th (Greater Poland) and 61st Regiments illustrate allegorically the fall of Prussia in World War 1.

The 60th (Greater Poland) was raised in Gostyn and the coat of arms of this town is part of the regimental badge.

The 32nd was a Masovian regiment and a badge similar in shape to that of the 86th was worn; the eagle in the latter holds the coat of arms of Mińsk.

Silesian eagles are present in the badges of the 73rd, 74th (Upper Silesia) and 75th Regiments, while Polish–Lithuanian and Samogitian emblems were part of the badges of the 76th and 77th. The 81st was named after the town of Grodno and the bow and arrow of Pińsk are shown in the badge of the 84th, a regiment from the region of Polesie. The badge of the 85th carries the Madonna of Ostra Brama (Wilno) in its centre.

Plate 24

1st (Legion) J. Piłsudski's Infantry Regiment
2nd, 3rd and 4th (Legion) Infantry Regiments
5th (Legion) J. Piłsudski's Zuchowatych Infantry Regiment
6th (Legion) J. Piłsudski's Infantry Regiment
7th, 8th and 9th (Legion) Infantry Regiments
10th, 11th, 12th and 13th Infantry Regiments
14th Ziemia Kujawska Infantry Regiment
15th Wilków Infantry Regiment
16th, 17th and 18th Infantry Regiments
19th Odsieczy Lwowa Infantry Regiment
20th Ziemia Krakowska Infantry Regiment
21st Warszawski Infantry Regiment
22nd Infantry Regiment
23rd Colonel L. Lis-Kula's Infantry Regiment
24th and 25th Infantry Regiments

Plate 25

26th and 27th Infantry Regiments
28th, 29th, 30th and 31st Kaniowski Rifle Regiments
32nd, 33rd, 34th and 35th Infantry Regiments
36th Academy Legion Infantry Regiment
37th Prince J. Poniatowski's Łęczyce Infantry Regiment
38th and 39th Lwowski Rifle Regiments
40th Dzieci Lwowskie Infantry Regiment
41st Marshal J. Piłsudski's Suwalski Infantry Regiment
42nd General J. H. Dąbrowski's Infantry Regiment
43rd Bayonne Legion Rifle Regiment
44th American Legion Rifle Regiment
45th and 48th Kresowy Rifles Infantry Regiments
49th Huculski Rifle Regiment

50th Francesco Nullo's Infantry Regiment
51st, 52nd, 53rd and 54th Kresowy Rifles Infantry Regiments
55th Poznański Infantry Regiment
56th Wielkopolski Infantry Regiment
57th King Carol II of Rumania's Infantry Regiment

Plate 26

58th Infantry Regiment
59th and 60th Wielkopolski Infantry Regiments
61st and 62nd Infantry Regiments
63rd Toruński Infantry Regiment
64th (Pomorski) Murmańsk Rifle Regiment
65th Starogardzki Infantry Regiment
66th Marshal J. Piłsudski's Kaszubski Infantry Regiment
67th, 68th and 69th Infantry Regiments
70th Infantry Regiment (12th Wielkopolski Rifle Regiment)
71st Infantry Regiment
72nd Colonel D. Czachowski's Infantry Regiment
73rd Infantry Regiment
74th Górnośląski Infantry Regiment
75th Infantry Regiment
76th L. Narbutt's Lidzki Infantry Regiment
77th, 78th, 79th and 80th Infantry Regiments
81st King Stefan Batory's Grodzieński Infantry Regiment
82nd T. Kościuszko's Syberyjski Rifle Regiment
83rd R. Traugutt's Poleski Rifle Regiment
84th Poleski Rifle Regiment
85th Wileński Rifle Regiment
86th Infantry Regiment

Plate 27. Highland Rifle Regiments and Rifle Battalions

The Highland Rifle Regiments were six in all and they belonged to the
21st and 22nd Mountain Divisions. The motifs in their badges are the
swastika, pine twigs and axe heads.

The enamel colours of the badge of the 1st Rifle Battalion were dark
blue and nile green, which were the colours of the collar patches of the
six rifle battalions. The griffin of Pomerania is depicted in the badge of
the 2nd Battalion.

The Marine Rifle Battalion was an Army unit, and thus there is an
army sword and the Polish eagle on a marine background in the centre of
its badge.

Cavalry (*Pl. 27 and 28*)

The Polish lancers were called Ułans, thus the 'U' is displayed in some badges. The cavalry badges are simpler in design than those of the infantry; most were in the shape of crosses. The officers' badges were made in coloured enamels that showed, in one way or the other, the colours of the regimental pennons. Some badges displayed the monogram worn on the shoulder straps and the majority displayed the Polish eagle. The 18th Lancers had the Pomeranian griffin as its centre and the 13th Lancers had the Madonna of Ostra Brama (centre).

Dark green was present in the pennons of all the Mounted Rifle Regiments and it also appeared in most of their regimental badges.

In 1939 the Polish cavalry was formed of the following regiments:

Plate 27.
1st J. Piłsudski's Light Horse Regiment
2nd Rokitniański Light Horse Regiment
3rd Colonel J. Kozietulski's Mazowiecki Light Horse Regiment
1st Colonel B. Mościcki's Krechowiecki Lancers Regiment
2nd General J. Dwernicki's Grochowski Lancers Regiment
3rd Śląski Lancers Regiment
4th Zaniemeński Lancers Regiment
5th Zasławski Lancers Regiment
6th Kaniowski Lancers Regiment
7th General K. Sosnkowski's Lubelski Lancers Regiment
8th Prince J. Poniatowski's Lancers Regiment
9th Małopolski Lancers Regiment
10th Litewski Lancers Regiment

Plate 28.
11th (Legion) Marshal E. Śmigły-Rydz's Lancers Regiment
12th Podolski Lancers Regiment
13th Wileński Lancers Regiment
14th Jazłowiecki Lancers Regiment
15th Poznański Lancers Regiment
16th General G. Orlicz-Dreszer's Wielkopolski Lancers Regiment
17th King Bolesław Chrobry's Wielkopolski Lancers Regiment
18th Pomorski Lancers Regiment
19th General E. Różycki's Wołynski Lancers Regiment
20th King Jan III Sobieski's Lancers Regiment
21st Nadwiślańskich Lancers Regiment
22nd Podkarpacki Lancers Regiment
23rd Grodzieński Lancers Regiment

24th Lancers Regiment
25th Wielkopolski Lancers Regiment
26th Hetman K. Chodkiewicz's Wielkopolski Lancers Regiment
27th King Stefan Batory's Lancers Regiment

1st and 2nd Mounted Rifles Regiments
3rd Hetman S. Czarnecki's Mounted Rifles Regiment
4th Ziemia Łęczycka Mounted Rifles Regiment
5th Mounted Rifles Regiment
6th Hetman S. Żółkiewski's Mounted Rifles Regiment
7th Wielkopolski Mounted Rifles Regiment
8th Mounted Rifles Regiment
9th General K. Pułaski's Mounted Rifles Regiment
10th Mounted Rifles Regiment

Plate 29. Field Artillery

The basic colours of the Field Artillery (Artyleria Lekka) badges were green and black. They were also the colours of their collar patches.

The first three were 'Legion' regiments as they were derived from the Polish artillery of World War 1. The 4th F.A. Regiment was named after the Kujawy region and the 5th was from Lwów.

The 8th 'Płocki' F.A. Regiment was dedicated to King Bolesław Krzywousty and the 10th 'Kaniowski' had the Cross of Kaniów in its badge. The 12th and 13th were named after the Kresy region; the 16th was a Pomeranian regiment and the 25th named after the region of Kalisz.

The 24th F.A. Regiment was dedicated to King Jan III Sobieski; the 26th to King Władysław IV.

There were thirty-one regiments of Field Artillery, but the 31st was never part of a division and was used as a training unit.

Plate 30. Artillery

The gunners of the Medium Artillery Regiments (Artyleria Ciężka) wore green and red collar patches, and the same colours are also present in their regimental badges.

The 2nd M.A. Regiment was named after the region of Chełmn and dedicated to Hetman J. Zamoyski. The 3rd was dedicated to King Stefan Batory and the 6th was nicknamed 'The Defenders of Lwów' and had the coat of arms of that town in its badge. The Polish Army included 10 Medium Artillery regiments.

There was one regiment of Heavy Artillery (Artyleria Najcięższa), of which the other ranks' badge is illustrated, and only one commemorative Horse Artillery badge, although each battery had its title and honorary leader.

The badge of the Survey Artillery, which was a specialised service composed of surveyors and rangefinders, was made in its colours of white and green enamel.

1st Marshal E. Śmigły-Rydz's A. A. Artillery Regiment wore a badge made in green and yellow enamel. Just before the outbreak of World War 2 another badge was adopted, made in bronze and worn by all A. A. Artillery units.

The badge of the 1st Motorised Artillery Regiment showed the 'anti-clockwise' swastika which the Polish Army adopted in the early 1930s. The green and black centre is enclosed in a cogwheel, the emblem of motorisation.

The last badge illustrated did not belong to the Artillery. It represents a profile of Marshal J. Piłsudski and was worn by Instructors of the Cadet Force.

Proficiency Badges
Although not strictly Army badges, the National Sports Badge (divided into three classes) and the Rifle Association Badge (which was divided into four classes) were both worn above the right breast pocket at the level of the first button. However, in the case of officers and warrant officers they were worn on the cross belt, just below the shoulder straps. There were also proficiency badges for equestrian skills, ski-ing and motoring.

Plate 31. Engineers and Signals
The breast pocket badges of the Polish Engineers, when made in coloured enamels, were generally in the Corps colours of black and red. Picks, shovels, axes and anchors were the symbols usually shown in the badges.

There were eight battalions in all, numbered 1 to 8, the 6th wearing the badge of the old 9th Battalion.

There were also separate badges for Railway and Bridging Battalions and a different red and black badge was worn by the Mounted Pioneers.

The Signals' officers' badges were made of black and cornflower blue enamels, most of them with the 'lightning' device associated with the Corps.

Personnel of the Electrotechnical Battalion wore a badge with the 'E' initial worn on the shoulder straps and the black and red colours of the Engineers on a background of 'electric' blue.

Plate 32. Armoured Troops
In 1939 the Polish Army had twelve armoured battalions, numbered from 1 to 12. (The 11th was an experimental battalion, attatched to the A.C.

Training Centre, and wore its badge.) Their badges depicted dragons, knights' helmets and other motifs appropriate to armour. The enamel colours were generally black and orange.

The 1st and 2nd Armoured Train Groups wore special badges, both with a knight's plumed helmet in the centre.

Services, Schools, etc.

The badge of the Inspectorate General of the Armed Forces was worn above the left breast pocket and showed the monogram of Marshal Piłsudski and the marshals' crossed batons on a blue background. All the other badges illustrated, with the exception of the grenade badge of the Military Police, were worn on the left breast pocket.

The Frontier Defence Corps, that garrisoned the eastern borders, was a regular army corps and came under the War Ministry, while the Border Guards that were deployed on the other borders were under the Ministry of the Interior. Both infantry and cavalry of the F.D.C. wore the same badge whose motto, 'Za Służbę Graniczną', means 'For Frontier Service'.

The Geographical Institute trained personnel of the Geographical Service who were employed in survey and mapping operations.

The Military Police (Żandarmeria) wore two badges: one badge was worn on the breast pocket and the other was worn only by policemen on actual policing duties. It hung on a chain fixed behind the collar on the left of the greatcoat, but above the medal ribbons on the tunic.

Additional Information

The badge for wounds was a ribbon half the width of that of the *Virtuti Militari* Cross; its ribbon was 4–7 cm long, with each wound represented by a silver star.

Front Service Stripes: they were worn on the upper right sleeve and were represented by inverted silver chevrons, one for each period of six months at the front.

Long Service Stripes (Regular Army): the stripes were normally worn by N.C.O.s on the upper left sleeve. The chevrons, in this case, were in silver braid with red edgings. One chevron was worn for each consecutive period of three years' service. A wider chevron was awarded on the 12th year and two wide chevrons were awarded for twenty-one years of service, together with normal narrower chevrons for the intermediate years of service.

Belgium

The Belgian military tradition goes back far beyond 1830, when national independence was gained.

In fact there were Belgian troops in the Austrian Army and, at the time of Napoleon, many Belgians took to his flag. At Waterloo there were Belgian units on both sides, some within Napoleon's army and others in Wellington's.

The Legion that fought for Napoleon was disbanded in 1815 when the territory of Belgium became part of the Kingdom of the Netherlands, and some infantry units were subsequently raised in the Netherlands, with a Belgian identity.

After the 1830 Revolution, on 14 October of that year, the National Congress proclaimed the Independence and, on 14 July of the following year, Prince Leopold of Saxe-Coburg became the first king of the Belgians. The new state was recognised internationally by the Treaty of London on 19 April, 1839.

After 1830, the new army was formed and there were French instructors who were responsible for the staff, while Polish instructors were mainly responsible for the raising and training of the cavalry units. Therefore, Lancers became part of the Belgian cavalry. The Guides regiment, which was one of the first cavalry units to be formed, originated from Cossack units which occupied Belgium during the Napoleonic wars.

In 1914, the corps and regiments of the Belgian Army wore their traditional uniforms, but later during the war khaki uniforms were introduced, with a steel helmet of French inspiration. The Belgian Lion's head was on the front of this helmet.

The khaki field uniform, although modernised in the 1930s, remained basically the same until World War 2. The rank badges were worn on the collar, in the form of stars and bars for officers and warrant officers, and on the forearms by the other ranks in the form of stripes.

Two different types of collar patches were worn on the jacket by officers and warrant officers. Generals, senior officers and advocates of the Legal Service wore collar patches 35 mm wide at the base, with an angle of 68° at the top; the other officers' and warrant officers' collar patches were 30 mm wide at the base, with a 72° angle at the top corner. The angles between the sides and the base were always of 98°. The height of the patch corresponded to the badges it contained.

Pointed collar patches were also worn on pointed collars as, for instance, on the leather tunic; they were made on an angle of 45°.

The officers wore khaki jackets while soldiers had tunics; all wore collar patches in the colours of their corps and services, and metal badges attached onto them if so required by regulations. The field cap was a characteristic forage cap with piping on the sides and along the top, and a tassel at the front. The piping and tassel were in the colour of the collar patches, and in gold or silver for the officers.

The Chasseurs of the Ardennes wore a dark green beret with the boar's head cap badge and the Border units a black beret with the wheel cap badge. In 1930, a dark blue full dress uniform was adopted for the officers. It consisted basically of a dark blue peaked cap, double-breasted tunic and trousers with large coloured stripes. Its style and piping colours varied according to different units.

Detachable shoulder cords were worn for parade and special duties, mainly on the khaki uniform. There were different types for generals, officers, warrant officers and regular N.C.O.s; the generals wore the Royal Cypher (King Leopold III, 1934–51) on the shoulder cords.

The Royal Cypher was also displayed on the buckle of the silk waist belt.

Plate 33. National Cockade, Cap Bands, Collar Patches and Shoulder Straps

All ranks of the Belgian Army wore a black, yellow and red cockade on the peaked cap.

The corps or service badge was also worn on the peaked cap, embroidered or pinned on the cap band, at the front over the chinstrap and various accoutrements showed the rank of the wearer.

Depending on their employment, generals were divided into three categories:

Generals of the Corps, who wore the badges illustrated here;

Generals of the Services, who kept the badges of their branch of service, adding general's stars and double bars on their particular collar badges;

Generals belonging to the cadre of Engineers of Military Productions (Military Supplies), who wore their badge representing a cogwheel superimposed on crossed hammers, and royal blue collar patches with scarlet piping.

All generals wore rank stars on the shoulder straps and, as already mentioned, the Royal Cypher badge on the shoulder cords.

Generals of the Corps wore the 'thunderbolt' badge (see Plate 38) on the cap and collar. On the peaked cap it was embroidered on an amaranth red band with twin vertical gold bars and gold piping. The chinstrap was formed by two sliding, smooth gold cords, of the pattern worn by all officers. They wore black collar patches with amaranth piping and the 'thunderbolt', stars and double bars embroidered in gold wire.

In 1939 there were two general's ranks as colonel-brigadiers wore colonel's badges with the addition of a scarlet red band on the cap. The gold belt buckle represented at the bottom of this plate was used by all officers, including generals.

Plates 34 and 35. Rank Badges

Officers

The cap band of the senior officers' peaked cap carried two single vertical gold bars and gold piping, while the only accoutrement granted to the junior officers' cap was a gold chinstrap. All cavalry units wore silver instead of gold.

Warrant officers wore silver badges and silver chinstrap cords on the peaked cap.

The rank badges worn on collar patches were represented by six-pointed stars (diam. 12 mm), embroidered or pinned on the patch at a distance of 15 mm one from the other, centre to centre.

One gold bar (30 mm × 7 mm), or two in the case of generals, was applied at the base of the patch in the case of a senior officer. A narrower bar was used as well for the rank badge of 1st captain and warrant officer 1st class and on its own, to denote the rank of 'clerk' of the Legal Service (Plate 35).

Captain-commandant or 1st captain refer to the same rank, some corps using one title, others the other.

The Belgian warrant officer was called 'adjutant', and wore stars and bars of silver.

Badges were worn on the headdress, on the collar of the jacket, tunic and greatcoat, and on the shoulder straps; the collar patches of the jacket and tunic being the common denominator, as they showed rank, colours of the corps or service, and often the corps or service's badge.

No collar patches were worn on the greatcoat collar, only badges embroidered or pinned directly on the collar itself.

Corps and Services

Represented in Plates 34 and Plate 35 are the patches of all Belgian corps and services as they were in 1939. I have illustrated these patches as they can be displayed by the collector. However, I am now going to describe them in the order of precedence applied by Belgian army regulations.

The corps and service badges were always worn, embroidered or pinned, on greatcoat collars but they were not necessarily worn on the collar patches as the colours of these were self-explanatory.

The badge of General Staff officers was, and still is, known as 'demi-foudre' and was worn on the cap, collar and shoulder straps. G.S. officers actually serving at the General Staff also wore an amaranth red arm band on the upper left arm, while G.S. officers attached to field units wore the unit's badge on the shoulder straps instead of the 'demi-foudre'.

For instance, a G.S. infantry officer stationed in the fortress of Namur, would be wearing the royal crown and Namur's garrison badge 'N' underneath on the shoulder straps.

§ The remaining patches are as follows:

Infantry of the Line: scarlet red collar patch with royal blue piping. Crown
Grenadiers: scarlet–royal blue. Grenade
Carabiniers: dark green–yellow. Bugle
Chasseurs on Foot: dark green–yellow. Crown
Chasseurs of the Ardennes: dark green–scarlet. Boar's head
Carbiniers Cyclists: dark green–yellow. Bicycle wheel
Frontier Cyclists Regiment: scarlet–royal blue. Bicycle wheel
Guides: amaranth red–green. Crown over crossed sabres
Lancers: white–royal blue. Crossed lances
Chasseurs on Horse: yellow–royal blue. Sabre across bugle
Light Horse: royal blue–scarlet. Grenade (with open flame)

Artillery		Crossed cannons
VII A. C. Artillery	royal blue–scarlet	Cogwheel on crossed cannons
Horse Artillery		Horse shoe and crossed cannons
Anti-Aircraft Artillery		Torch, crossed cannons and wings

Engineers: *black–scarlet. Roman helmet

Transport Corps: ultramarine blue–royal blue. Car wheel

Doctors: *amaranth–amaranth	
Pharmacists: *emerald green–green	Caduceus within wreath
Dentists: *dark violet–amaranth	
Veterinaries: *ultramarine–royal blue	

Medical Service (O.R.): amaranth–royal blue. Caduceus

Commissaries: royal blue–sky blue. Caduceus of Mercury
N.C.O.s Secretaries of Commissariat: royal blue–grey blue. 'S' and 'I' interlaced
as above but attached to Army Corps: royal blue–grey blue. Letter 'I'

* Denotes velvet; all other patches were in felt

Officers Administrative
Secretaries, N.C.O. Archivist } royal blue–ultramarine.
and Treasury Secretaries: } 'S' and 'A' interlaced

Administrative Officers: royal blue–grey blue. Letter 'A'

Judge Advocate Generals
Judge Advocates } royal blue–ultramarine (see badges below)
Clerks

Members of the Legal Service did not wear the usual army ranks. There
were only two officers' ranks, both represented by a 7 mm gold bar on
the collar. Small differences in their badges further distinguished the two
ranks, i.e. Judge Advocate Generals were entitled to an oak wreath while
Judge Advocates wore a laurel wreath around the badge. Clerks of the
Courts wore the *faisceau de licteur* without a wreath (Plate 38).

Officers of the } royal blue–grey blue. Cogwheel on crossed
Military Supplies: } hammers

Officers Supplies
Accountants and } royal blue–grey blue. Letter 'M'
Quartermasters N.C.O.s

Sergeants and Corporals

Sergeants and bandsmen of the regular army wore a peaked cap with
white metal badges and a leather chinstrap, while corporals and privates
were entitled to wear the peaked cap only after respectively ten and fifteen
years of active service. Their chinstrap was faced with khaki material.

The rank stripes were of silver braid for sergeants and red for corporals,
worn on the forearms over the cuffs, pointing inwards at a 30° angle. Both
sergeants' and corporals' stripes were 50 mm long and 5 mm in depth.

Plate 36. Officers' Badges on Peaked Cap, Jacket and Greatcoat

Officers wore their corps or service badges on the cap and greatcoat collar
and often on the collar patches.

The badges on the shoulder straps had not necessarily to be the same,
as they represented the unit the officer was attached to at the moment.
The same rule applies to all the other ranks.

This plate, for instance, shows the badges worn by a lieutenant-colonel
of Artillery attached to the Engineers and Fortifications Headquarters.

He thus wore the Engineer's helmet and the fortress badge on the shoulder straps.

The other set of badges relate to those worn by a lieutenant doctor of the Medical Service attached to the 2nd Grenadier Regiment.

Grenadiers serving in grenadiers regiments did not wear the crown on the shoulder straps.

Infantrymen and Chasseurs of the Ardennes wore only the crown with the regimental number underneath on the shoulder straps; Carabiniers wore the crown, the bugle and the regimental number, while Chasseurs on Foot wore the crown and the bugle with the number in its centre.

The crown over the bicycle wheel with regimental number was worn by the Frontier Cyclists Regiment.

Guides wore the crown over the regimental number on the shoulder straps. Grenade and number were worn by cavalrymen of Light Horse regiments. Lancers and Chasseurs on Horse wore only the regimental number.

However, if a doctor, for instance, became attached to a regiment of Chasseurs on Horse, he would wear the 'bugle and sabre' badge as well as the regimental number on the shoulder straps, because in this case the regimental number would not be enough to identify his unit. Troops of any corps or service attached to the cavalry divisions wore the crossed sabres on the shoulder straps.

Gunners wore only the regimental numbers, except those serving with Army Artillery (Heavy), who also wore the crossed cannons, or those serving with the VII Army Corps (motorised) Anti-Aircraft Depot or in the Artillery Repair Service, who wore the appropriate badges as well as the unit's number.

Artillery units stationed at the Namur and Liège Fortresses wore the 'N' or 'L' badges under the crown.

Sappers generally wore the battalion's number on the shoulder straps but when attached to other units, as they more often are, they wore that unit's badge. For instance, sappers attached to the Chasseurs of the Ardennes Division wore the boar's head and the divisional number. Specialised Engineers units wore their own particular badges.

Troops of the Corps of Transport, with 'car wheel' badge on the cap and Transport's collar patch, wore the badge of the units they were attached to on the shoulder straps while, vice-versa, an officer of the Administrative Service attached to the Corps of Transport would be wearing the 'car wheel' badge on shoulder straps.

Plate 37. Corps and Service Badges
The badges illustrated in this and the following plate could be found embroidered in gold or silver wire, in white metal or brass.

The Belgian infantry was divided into: Infantry of the Line, Grenadiers, Carabiniers, Chasseurs on Foot, Chasseurs of the Ardennes. Carabiniers Cyclists, the Frontier Cyclists Regiment and any other unit of cyclists wore a badge representing a bicycle wheel.

The cavalry was composed of regiments of Guides, Lancers, Chasseurs on Horse and regiments of Light Horse.

Two crossed cannons were the symbol of artillery, but gunners serving in the Cavalry Corps, or Cavalry Divisions, had a horseshoe added to the crossed guns. The Artillery of the VII Army Corps had a cogwheel superimposed on the cannons; the Anti-Aircraft Artillery and the Artillery Repair Service were entitled to particular badges of their own.

The badge 'R' of the Cavalry Depot stands for *Remonte*, and 'P', an artillery badge, stands for *Parc d'artillerie*. The roman helmet was the badge of the engineers, but specialised engineering units wore different badges on the shoulder straps. The crossed axes was the badge of the *Pontonniers*, the winged wheel that of the Military Railways, the letter 'F', standing for *Fontainiers* the service of water suppliers. Signal troops and the Camouflage Service also wore different badges.

Independent from the Corps of Transport, there was the Headquarters of Transport (*Direction des Transports*). Its badge clearly explains its role by representing, as a whole, the badges of the road, river and railway transportation systems.

'I' stands for '*Intendance*', or the Commissariat Service.

Plate 38. Corps and Service Badges and Numerals

Chaplains had three different badges depending which religion they represented. Other ranks of the Medical, Veterinary and Pharmacist Services wore a badge similar to that of the officers, the caduceus, but without wreath.

Civilian personnel attached to the Armed Forces wore the Belgian Lion on the headdress and collar of their uniform. Generals, however, did not wear the amaranth red band on the peaked cap. Civilian personnel also wore a black, yellow and red armband on the left upper arm, with their name, surname and service to which they were attached on the reverse.

Civilian personnel serving in the Military Railway Service, Telegraphic and Telephone Service, wore the metallic letters C.F.T. on a 7 mm × 54 mm patch of green material, stitched on the armband.

Roman numerals represented army corps numbers, arabic numerals were reserved for battalion, regimental and divisional numbers.

'Attributes des Fonctions'

The badges illustrated at the bottom half of plate 38 are badges of 'functions' or duties (*Attributes des Fonctions*). They show the appointment of an officer or N.C.O. and therefore, in the Belgian army regulations, are always shown grouped apart from the others.

They were all worn on the cap, as well as on the collar and shoulder straps.

Auxiliary troops wore the scarlet and royal blue infantry collar patches, the royal crown on the peaked cap and, on the forage cap and shoulder straps, the roman helmet, with regimental number below, in roman numerals.

Personnel of the services not listed above wore the headdress badges of their previous corps or service.

Cap Badges of Regiments in Plate 37 and 38

	Forage Cap and Beret	*Peaked Cap*
Infantry of the Line	crown regimental number	crown
Grenadiers	grenade regimental number	grenade
Carabiniers	bugle regimental number	bugle
Chasseurs on Foot	crown regimental number	crown
Chasseurs of the Ardennes	boar's head regimental number	boar's head
Carabiniers Cyclists	bicycle wheel regimental number	bicycle wheel
Frontier Cyclists Regt	crown bicycle wheel	bicycle wheel
Guides	crown crossed sabres regimental number	crown crossed sabres
Lancers	crossed lances regimental number	crossed lances
Chasseurs on Horse	sabre across bugle regimental number	sabre and bugle
Light Horse	grenade regimental number	grenade

	Forage Cap and Beret	*Peaked Cap*
Artillery	crossed cannons regimental number	crossed cannons
VII Anti-Aircraft Artillery	cogwheel on crossed cannons	
Horse Artillery	horse shoe–crossed cannons regimental number	horse shoe–crossed cannons
Anti-Aircraft Artillery	torch-wings–crossed cannons regimental number	torch-wings–crossed cannons
Fortress Artillery	crown crossed cannons	
Artillery Repair Service	compass and lightnings	
Engineers	roman helmet	
Engineers Battalions	roman helmet battalion number	roman helmet
Transport Corps	car wheel	
Doctors, Pharmacists, Dentists, Veterinaries	caduceus within wreath	
Medical Service (O.R.)	caduceus	
Commissaries	caduceus of Mercury	
N.C.O.s Secretaries of Commissariat	'S' and 'I' interlaced	
as above but attached to A. C. and field units	letter 'I'	
Officers Administrative Secretaries, N.C.O.s Archivist and Treasury Secretaries	'S' and 'A' interlaced	
Administrative Officers	letter 'A'	
Judge Advocate Generals	*faisceau de licteur* within oak wreath	
Judge Advocates	*faisceau de licteur* within laurel wreath	
Clerks	*faisceau de licteur*	
Catholic Chaplains	Latin cross	
Protestant Chaplains	Maltese cross	
Jewish Rabbis	Star of David	

	Forage Cap and Beret	*Peaked Cap*
Officers of the Military Supplies		cogwheel on crossed hammers
Officers Supplies Accountants and Quartermaster N.C.O.s		letter 'M'
Civilian personnel attached to the Armed Forces		Belgian lion

Italy

For centuries, Italy was divided into several independent states. It was finally united in 1861 by the House of Savoy, whose kings, through war and diplomacy, succeeded in taking over all the remainder of the Italian peninsula.

The origins of the House of Savoy are lost in the past. At the beginning of the eleventh century, Umberto Biancamano, Count of Aosta, ruled over Savoy, Maurienne, Belley and, of course, Aosta. Having control of the Alpine passes between France and Italy, the Savoy rulers were constantly involved in the wars between neighbouring countries. In 1416, Emperor Sigismund made Amedeus VIII a duke. At the Peace of Utrecht, the House of Savoy obtained the island of Sicily, and became a monarchy. But in 1720, King Victor Amedeus II exchanged Sicily for Sardinia, and henceforth the rulers became Kings of Sardinia.

In 1557, Duke Emmanuel Philibert (known as 'Ironhead') began to organise his feudal militias into a number of companies, under the command of captains, with 400 men to each company. A regiment was made up of six companies, commanded by a colonel appointed by the Duke.

By Royal Decree of 19 October, 1664, the infantry regiments adopted the name of the province in which they were recruited, instead of, as formerly, being referred to by their colonel's name or by French titles of Savoyard derivation.

As early as 1626, barracks were built and in 1671 troops were given their first uniforms, a blue sash having been the only common distinguishing feature of the Army since 1572.

The uniforms of the Sardinian Army, and later those of the Italian Army, tended to follow the pattern of those of neighbouring France.

The region of Savoy and Nice were lost to France after the French Revolution, and in 1801 Piedmont also was annexed by France. It became the 27th French Territorial division, recruiting for the 111th Infantry Regiment, 31st Light Infantry, 21st Dragoons and 26th Light Horse of the Imperial Army. Several legions of Italian volunteers also followed the fortunes of Napoleon, with the green, white and red cockade as their national emblem.

The Congress of Vienna re-established the Kingdom of Sardinia to the status it had had before the French Revolution, and the remainder of Italy came under the Austrian sphere of influence.

King Charles Albert (1831–49) waged war with Austria but was defeated in both the 1848 and 1849 campaigns. His successor, Victor

Emmanuel II (1849–78), conducted the Second and Third Wars of Independence and successfully unified all the Italian States under the Savoy crown. In 1861 the Kingdom of Sardinia became the Kingdom of Italy and, in 1870, Rome became its capital.

The grey-green field uniform was adopted in 1909 and consisted basically of a soft cap (*kepi*) and a tunic with a high collar and four pockets for the officers (pocketless for the other ranks). Officers and mounted troops wore breeches with boots or leggings; the remainder of the army wore trousers and puttees.

After World War 1, in 1923, new dress regulations were published by which four patch pockets were added at last to the other ranks' tunics. Stripes were added onto the seams of the officers' breeches. Unfortunately, at the same time, the other ranks' trousers were replaced by ugly plus-fours.

New regulations modified the Italian uniform yet again in 1933. The high collar was replaced by a more comfortable open collar; the peaked cap and a field cap called *bustina* (little envelope) were issued to all ranks.

In 1935 a new type of helmet, initially with a small crest, replaced the French type adopted during World War 1.

Officers were entitled to wear three uniforms: black for special duties; white, ordinarily worn during summer; and grey-green, the only uniform most officers owned. However, alternated with different headdresses (peaked cap, field cap and helmet), with metal decorations or ribbons, different shoulder boards or epaulettes, etc., these three uniforms could be adapted into several forms of dress, depending upon the duties performed by an officer.

Until 1889, the 'colonial' uniform was white for all ranks, but a new khaki uniform was then introduced, redder in tone than British khaki.

Other ranks also wore a grey cotton garrison uniform, the jacket having side pockets only on which no badges were worn, except collar stars and N.C.O.s' chevrons.

The arms and corps of the Italian Army were distinguished from each other by different colours, worn on the uniform in the form of piping or facing on the collar, cuffs, etc.

The colours were:

Infantry, Grenadiers	scarlet
Medical Corps and Pharmacists	amaranth red
Bersaglieri (Rifle regiments), Engineers	crimson
Alpini (Mountain Infantry)	green
Artillery	yellow
Veterinary Corps	light blue
Motor Transport, Administrative and Supply Corps	blue

General Staff	turquoise blue
Commissariat	violet
Fencing Instructors	white

Cavalry regiments had piping and facing in the regimental colours.

On the white and khaki uniforms the coloured piping was around the shoulder boards only.

The tunic of the officers' black uniform was double-breasted with two rows of buttons, pointed cuffs and a folded collar buttoned up to the neck.

The collars and cuffs were generally made of black velvet, edged with coloured piping (Infantry, Artillery, Engineers, Supply and Administrative Corps), but officers of specialised corps (Doctors, Pharmacists, Veterinaries, Commissaries and General Staff Officers) wore collars made entirely of coloured velvets.

Alpini and *Bersaglieri* had coloured cuffs and wore their flames on a black velvet collar. Grenadiers wore silver 'double bars' on both the red cloth collar and the cuffs.

The officers of the Tank Corps wore red 'flames' on a black collar, and the Motor Transport Corps black 'flames' on a blue collar.

Coloured stripes were also worn on the trousers.

The headdress of the grey-green uniform for officers and other ranks alike was a peaked cap, a field cap or a steel helmet. Special troops were issued with different types of headdress as well.

Bersaglieri wore a wide-brimmed black hat with a cluster of cockerel feathers, or a crimson felt fez with a blue tassel, the latter taking the place of the field cap.

All mountain troops wore the traditional feathered hat: officers wore a gilded feather holder; other ranks had an oval woollen pompon instead, each battalion having a different colour. Senior officers wore a white goose feather, junior officers an eagle feather and other ranks a crow feather.

Dragoons wore their own traditional crested helmet, while Lancers and the rest of the Cavalry wore sealskin caps.

All ranks of the Horse Artillery were issued with a stiff grey-green kepi with a black leather visor.

The officers' tunic was grey-green with open collar and four patch pockets. The shoulder boards and the cuffs were edged with coloured piping and the upper part of the collar was faced or piped in much the same way as the collar of the black uniform. An exception was made for the infantry where all ranks wore the regimental patch instead of red piping on the collar. The collar itself was made of black velvet for officers and that of other ranks was faced with black felt.

Officers had grey-green breeches with 2 cm black double stripes and coloured central piping; warrant officers also wore breeches but they had only a narrow coloured piping along the seams. The other ranks wore facings only on the upper part of the collar, under the patch or 'flame', without any pipings.

The *Guardia alla Frontiera* (Frontier Guard) was raised in 1934. All ranks wore a green cap band on the peaked cap and green facing on the upper part of the collar. The infantry of the Border Guard wore additional red piping, the engineers, crimson, and the artillery, yellow.

In the late 1930s, a number of armoured and motorised divisions were formed and all troops attached to these wore the upper part of the collar faced with blue felt and the collar patches and 'flames' superimposed onto it.

Plate 39. Generals' Rank Badges

Owing to the great numbers of World War I officers reaching higher ranks, and to the enormous numerical expansion of the Army, it became necessary, in the mid-thirties, to adopt new ranks for generals. The rank of general 'in command' of an army denotes that the wearer was an Army Corps general, detailed to command an army.

After the conquest of Ethiopia, King Victor Emmanuel III became Emperor and, together with Mussolini, his military rank became that of First Marshal of the Empire. The title of an Italian field general always referred to the unit he was in command of, i.e. General of Army, General of Army Corps, etc. Generals of army services who did not command field units had titled ranks (major general, etc.).

The generals' cap badge was the crowned eagle of Savoy, that centuries before had been used on the regimental banners; it was embroidered in gold wire for marshals, generals of army and generals of Army Corps, and in silver for all the others.

The generals' cap badge was embroidered on red felt; General Staff officers wore the same cap badge, but embroidered in gold on grey-green.

Generals of the Medical Corps and of the Commissariat wore their cap badges embroidered on the colour of the Corps, and generals of the Legal Corps wore all their badges on grey-green instead of red.

The typical ornament of the generals' rank badge was called a *greca*, a simplification of the traditional embroideries worn by Piedmontese generals in the Sardinian Army.

It was embroidered on the band of the peaked cap with one additional silver stripe for brigadiers, two for Division and Army Corps generals (the latter with gold cap badge). There were three silver stripes for generals of Army and four for marshals of Italy. The First Marshal of the Empire wore two *greche* on the cap band.

The same pattern was followed for rank badges worn on the jacket or greatcoat, with additional crowns and batons in gold for certain ranks. As these rank badges were rather cumbersome on the field cap, in 1935 stars were adopted as rank badges, for generals and all other officers alike.

The rank badges on the sleeves were worn over the cuffs, and were embroidered on cherry red for medical generals, on violet for commissariat generals and on grey-green for all other generals.

Shoulder boards and metal epaulettes are not illustrated in this book because they are considered parts of the uniform, rather than badges. Epaulettes were in silver and shoulder boards in silver braid, with red backing; gold stars, and a smaller replica of the cap badge, were embroidered in the centre. Generals of the three Army Corps mentioned above wore a small replica of the corps' cap badge instead.

Plate 40. Officers' Rank Badges

Officers also had their rank badges on the headdress and, normally, on both forearms of the jacket. In the case of the black uniform, white summer uniform and colonial uniform, such badges were worn on the shoulder boards instead of on the forearms. Gold embroidered stars (with a small bar at the outside end of the shoulder board in the case of 1st Lieutenant or 1st Captain) were worn by junior officers; the same by senior officers but with an additional 6 mm gold braid stripe (called *millerighe*) around the edges. A small replica of the cap badge was also attached in the centre of the shoulder board. Black shoulder boards were worn with black and colonial uniforms, and grey-green shoulder boards with grey-green and white uniforms.

Colonel regimental commanders wore all badges on red (a brick red called *robbio*) backing; unassigned colonels wore them on grey-green, as did other officers. A colonel 'in command' of a Brigade wore colonel's badges (on red) on the forearms and on the band of the peaked cap, and a silver general's cap badge and small silver eagle on the shoulder boards in place of stars.

The officers' badges were gold braid stripes, 10 mm in depth, on the forearms, the top stripe being adapted into a loop. A 17 mm gold stripe was the basic insignia of senior rank, a thin black woven gold-edged stripe, that of cadets.

Any officer 'in charge' of a superior command had a red patch inside the loop of the rank badges; a gold star inside the loop showed that the officer, of any rank, was an adjutant.

The rank of 1st captain, or 1st lieutenant, was given to officers after twelve years' service as a captain or lieutenant, or after twenty years' commission. They wore a small gold star under the rank badges, stitched onto the cuffs.

During the war, all rank badges became smaller and later, instead of gold, they were made in yellow silk.

The rank badges of medical officers and commissaries are stitched onto a rectangular backing felt which was in the colour of their particular service. Chaplains wore their badges on purple backing.

Plate 41. Warrant Officers' Rank Badges

The Italian warrant officer was, and is still, called a *maresciallo*. There were three ranks which were represented by stripes of a special gold braid which, in one, two or three stripes, were stitched onto the shoulder boards as illustrated.

From September, 1917, for the duration of the war, a new warrant officer's rank was granted for exceptional acts of valour performed by other ranks. Indeed, any warrant officer, N.C.O. or soldier could be granted the rank of *Aiutante di battaglia* on the field. At the end of the war each of them was given a premium of 200 lire for each month of service with such a rank. The sum could not exceed 1,400 lire. During World War 2 the rank consisted of three stripes of warrant officer's braid on red backing, forming a loop around the button. No *Aiutanti di battaglia* were made during World War 2, so nowadays this rank could be considered defunct.

All warrant officers, regardless of their rank, wore, and still wear, one stripe of W.O.'s braid, slightly larger than that mentioned above, around the band of the peaked cap, or a 60 mm stripe on the field cap.

Non-commissioned Officers and Other Ranks

In the Italian Army, only sergeants and sergeant-majors are termed N.C.O.s; they wore gold chevrons, while corporals wore black woven chevrons on both forearms, over the cuffs. Before World War 2 these chevrons were adopted, in shorter, inverted form, on the upper sleeves, and later, during the war, corporals and corporal-majors were issued with red chevrons.

Such chevrons were all woven as a ribbon, then cut and sewn in 'V' form on grey-green material, ready to be stitched onto the sleeves of the wearer. During World War 2 they became smaller and smaller, the gold ones being replaced by yellow woven chevrons.

Sergeants and corporals did not wear any rank badges other than those on the sleeves.

Plate 42. Collar Patches

Italian collar patches are specifically those of rectangular shape while the pointed patches are called 'flames'. They originated from the coloured facings and trimmings worn on the uniforms of the old Sardinian Army.

In the mid-1930s these colours once again became part of the uniform but, when all linings, facings and pipings were abolished in 1940, the 'colours' were restricted to the actual patches. They were worn by all ranks on the collar of the jacket.

According to regulations, the infantry collar patches should have been 60 mm long but as the war went on they became smaller and smaller. The patch illustrated was that of the 291st/292nd *Zara* Infantry Brigade.

By the Royal Warrant of 3 October, 1815, the infantry regiments of the Sardinian Army were 'brigaded' in twos under the same title. The Brigade remained the basic infantry formation ever after. In 1935, a field artillery regiment and support services were attached to each brigade, thus creating an infantry division. From about 1940 the divisional artillery, engineers, medical, administrative and supply units wore their 'flames' sewn onto the collar patch of the divisional infantry.

The cavalry regiments had three-pointed flames, often with coloured edgings; in the case of cavalry Scout Groups attached to infantry divisions, the flames were sewn on the collar patch of the divisional infantry.

The grenadiers of the *Granatieri di Sardegna* Division wore silver or white 'double bars' on a red patch; those of the *Granatieri di Savoia* wore the bars on a royal blue patch, red and royal blue having been the colours of their collars and cuffs during the 1930s.

In the same period all the troops belonging to armoured and motorised divisions were wearing their flames on blue collars: and so in 1940 they adopted their own collar patches by sewing the flames on rectangular blue backgrounds. For a short time in 1940 the armoured artillery wore a blue flame with yellow edging.

The infantry of the *Trento* and *Trieste* (illustrated) Motorised Divisions wore a half infantry patch sewn on a rectangular blue background. Machine-gunners wore two types of patches, both on blue backgrounds.

The first units of Light Tanks were raised on the 19th (Guides) Cavalry Regiment which had three-pointed flames on their blue collar. To commemorate this association, a similar collar patch was adopted, but with two-pointed flames on a blue rectangular background.

Personnel of the Transport Corps wore one-pointed orange flames, but for the newly-formed Motor Transport Corps black flames on blue collar were adopted and subsequently, black flames on blue patches.

In the 1930s, the officers of the Alpine artillery and engineers had worn artillery or engineers' uniforms and were distinguished as mountain troops only by the badges on the headdress and shoulder boards. In 1940 they adopted the flames previously worn by the other ranks, now on rectangular green patches. However, the artillery of the *Julia* Division temporarily adopted green flames with yellow edging, and they were still wearing them during the Greek campaign.

Parachutists of the parachute divisions, personnel of the Chemical Centre and *Guastatori* (Assault engineers) had large, embroidered collar patches, the latter replacing them in 1940 with normal engineers' flames; the sword and flaming grenade was, by then, worn as an arm badge.

The patch of general staff officers could be worn stitched on other collar patches when the officer was posted to a unit. Adjutants wore crowned stars on the collar instead of the usual stars.

All personnel of the Fascist Militia wore two-pointed black flames: the *fascio* was made of gilt for officers; in silver or white metal for N.C.O.s and brass for the other ranks. Personnel of the 'M' (Mussolini's) Battalions, raised in the early 1940s, wore a red 'M' on the flames across the *fascio*.

Cap Badges (*Pl. 43, 44, 45*)

Traditionally the infantry, cavalry and service corps connected with them, wore silver badges, except for the *Bersaglieri* who wore gold. Artillery and engineers, in the old days known as 'skilled' corps, also wore gold.

With the introduction of the 1933 army regulations, gold was granted to all the Army, except, as we have seen, the generals, who kept to their traditional silver badges.

Officers, warrant officers and non-commissioned officers wore gold wire, hand-embroidered cap badges; corporals and soldiers brass or machine embroidered badges in black rayon.

There were two sizes of embroidered badges: a large size worn by officers (W.O. and N.C.O.) on the peaked cap, embroidered on grey-green, black or brick red felt, and on khaki material for colonial uniform. A cap badge embroidered on grey-green was also worn on the white summer cap as the band was grey-green.

The field cap badge was smaller and should not be confused with the badges worn on the shoulder boards which were generally smaller still. It was embroidered in gold for officers (W.O. and N.C.O.) and black rayon for other ranks.

Some large brass cap badges were worn on the other rank's peaked cap before World War 2. These same badges were previously worn on the tricolor cockade of the nineteenth century blue *kepi*, and had always been worn on the colonial helmet.

Plate 43.
The cap badges in this and the two following plates are those worn by officers (W.O. and N.C.O.), embroidered in gold and used during the period 1933–43.

Cap badges of corps that were divided into regiments had a black velvet centre where the regimental number was applied or, in the case of un-assigned officers, a cross.

The infantry cap badge was adopted by officers around 1907 and by other ranks in the early twenties. The former was at that time in silver, the latter the same size as that of the officers, but embroidered in black wool.

Officers' cap badges with red centres and other rank's metal cap badges with red numerals belonged to regiments stationed in the colonies.

The first companies of *Bersaglieri* were raised in 1836 for light infantry duties and until 1870 they wore the battalion number in the cap badge (from 1 to 50). During World War 1, twenty-one regiments of *Bersaglieri* were raised.

The Colonial Rifles were raised in July, 1887 in Eritrea under the name *Cacciatori d'Africa*; their cap badge, a mixture of infantry and *Bersaglieri* designs, could also be found with a green or red centre.

The infantry of the *Trento* and the *Trieste* Motorised Divisions wore a particular cap badge with a cogwheel around the centre. Paratroopers were granted the winged dagger cap badge just before World War 2, the blade of the dagger often being embroidered in silver.

In 1936 light tanks and armoured cars were detached from the Tank Corps to form three groups (S. Marco, S. Giusto and S. Martino) of so-called 'fast' tanks, each group later joining one of the three *Celere* Divisions.

The first four regiments of the Italian cavalry have always traditionally been Dragoons. During World War 1 there also existed eight regiments of Lancers and eighteen regiments of Cavalry, but after the war, most were disbanded. Thus only representative regiments of dragoons, lancers and cavalry saw service during World War 2 still wearing their traditional cap badges.

The 10th Assault Regiment was an independent parachute unit whose members underwent special training for 'commando' type operations.

The Motor Transport Corps changed its cap badge in the mid-1930s as the badge initially adopted symbolised railway transport instead of motor transport. Nevertheless the former badge was kept in use, worn by transport units without motorisation.

Plate 44.

In the mid-thirties the old Heavy, Medium and Field Artillery were renamed Army, Army Corps and Divisional Artillery and, at the same time, Motorised Artillery came into being, as part of the Motorised Divisions.

Coast Artillery and most of the Anti-Aircraft Artillery batteries were taken over by the Fascist Territorial Militia while Light Artillery and Train Artillery were disbanded.

The Royal Corps of Engineers was established in 1752, fortification works and engineering previously having been carried out by artillery units. The first Pioneer battalion, of six companies of pioneers and one of miners, was formed in 1816, and the first regiment in 1859. The Regiment (4th) of Bridging Engineers was formed by companies of bridging specialists and the so-called *lagunari*, who were trained for amphibious engineering and stationed near Venice.

The first signal units were part of the Corps of the Engineers and, before World War 1, they were granted the sappers' cap badge with the addition of small lightnings around the grenade, as a symbol of electric sparks.

Railway Engineers and Miners have always been highly specialised sections of the Corps and, although they possessed their independent training depots, were not regimented but, usually at company strength, were attached to the larger formations.

Plate 45.

The Colonial Mounted Rifles were raised together with the *Cacciatori d'Africa* in 1887, of which they were the supporting cavalry.

In 1873, the Corps of Military Intendance became the Corps of Commissaries or Commissariat, formed only of officers, with the duty of superintending the supply and administration of the Army. Doctors of the Medical Corps, veterinaries, pharmacists, commissaries of the Red Cross, chaplains and lawyers of the Legal Corps were all officers. Fencing instructors, however, were all 2nd Lieutenants.

The first fifteen companies of *Alpini* were formed by Army Order of 15 October, 1872 and by 1882 there already existed six regiments which by 1909 became eight, totalling twenty-six battalions.

In the meantime, regiments of mountain gunners and companies of pioneers, miners and signalmen were also raised in support of the infantry. The Alpine battalions were never numbered but named instead after the town, mountain, village or valley in the battalion's recruiting area.

A small enamel badge, a different one for each battalion, was also worn on the hat near the feather holder.

Infantry, Artillery and Engineers wore different cap badges, adopted before World War 1. They are still in use today. The *Alpini* cap badge, like the other soldiers' cap badges, was black rayon on worsted. The pattern worn during World War 2 is illustrated in Plate 46.

The Frontier Guard (*Guardia alla Frontiera*) was raised in 1934 and its members wore the mountain troops' hat, with coloured feather holder but without a feather. Divided into infantry, artillery and engineers, they wore the corresponding badges, but with a green centre and roman, instead of arabic, numerals. The Frontier Guard was divided into 'sectors' and not regiments. Machine-gunners wore the special badge of an eagle clutching a machine-gun.

Italian Divisions of World War 2

A list of World War 2 divisions is given in the following pages. A number of these took part in the Abyssinian campaign under a different name or number.

It should be noted that most of the infantry divisions were named after their infantry brigade; in other cases both titles are given. Although this is an official list, by 1943 the greater part of these infantry divisions were only partially formed, others existed only on paper.

The armoured and motorised divisions were all destroyed in North Africa and so was the *Folgore* Parachute Division. The Alpine divisions were employed on all fronts except the North African and the *Celere* divisions were split up and eventually their units were destroyed on the North African and Russian fronts.

Infantry Divisions

No.	Title	Infantry Regiments	Artillery Regiment
13th	RE	1st–2nd	23rd
29th	PIEMONTE	3rd–4th	24th
28th	AOSTA	5th–6th	22nd
6th	CUNEO	7th–8th	27th
50th	REGINA	9th–10th	50th
56th	CASALE	11th–12th	56th
24th	PINEROLO	13th–14th	18th
55th	SAVONA	15th–16th	12th
33rd	ACQUI	17th–18th	33rd
27th	BRESCIA	19th–20th	55th
44th	CREMONA	21st–22nd	7th
14th	ISONZO	23rd–24th (COMO Bde)	6th
15th	BERGAMO	25th–26th	4th
17th	PAVIA	27th–28th	26th
26th	ASSIETTA	29th–30th (PISA Bde)	25th
51st	SIENA	31st–32nd	51st
4th	LIVORNO	33rd–34th	28th
16th	PISTOIA	35th–36th	30th
3rd	RAVENNA	37th–38th	121st
25th	BOLOGNA	39th–40th	205th
37th	MODENA	41st–42nd	29th
36th	FORLI'	43rd–44th	36th

No.	Title	Infantry Regiments	Artillery Regiment	
30th	SABAUDA	45th–46th (REGGIO Bde)	16th	
23rd	FERRARA	47th–48th	14th	
49th	PARMA	49th–50th	49th	
22nd	CACCIATORI DELLE ALPI	51st–52nd	1st	
2nd	SFORZESCA	53rd–54th (UMBRIA Bde)	17th	
32nd	MARCHE	55th–56th	32nd	
10th	PIAVE	57th–58th (ABBRUZZI Bde)	20th	
102nd	TRENTO (Mot.)	61st–62nd (SICILIA Bde)	46th	7th Bersaglieri Regt.
59th	CAGLIARI	63rd–64th	59th	
101st	TRIESTE (Mot.)	65th–66th (VALTELLINA Bde)	21st	9th Bersaglieri Regt.
58th	LEGNANO	67th–68th (PALERMO Bde)	58th	
61st	SIRTE	69th–70th (ANCONA Bde)	43rd	
38th	PUGLIE	71st–72nd	15th	
57th	LOMBARDIA	73rd–74th	57th	
54th	NAPOLI	75th–76th	54th	
7th	LUPI DI TOSCANA	77th–78th	30th	
9th	PASUBIO	79th–80th (ROMA Bde)	8th	
52nd	TORINO	81st–82nd	52nd	
19th	VENEZIA	83rd–84th	19th	
60th	SABRATHA	85th–86th (VERONA Bde)	42nd	
20th	FRIULI	87th–88th	35th	
5th	COSSERIA	89th–90th (SALERNO Bde)	29th	
1st	SUPERGA	91st–92nd (BASILICATA Bde)	5th	
18th	MESSINA	93rd–94th	2nd	
103rd	PIACENZA	111th–112th	37th	
104th	MANTOVA	113th–114th	11th	
62nd	MARMARICA	115th–116th (TREVISO Bde)	44th	
155th	EMILIA	119th–120th	155th	

No.	Title	Infantry Regiments	Artillery Regiment
153rd	MACERATA	121st–122nd	153rd
80th	SPEZIA (Airborne)	125th–126th	80th
41st	FIRENZE	127th–128th	41st
151st	PERUGIA	129th–130th	151st
47th	BARI	139th–140th	47th
64th	CATANZARO	141st–142nd	203rd
12th	SASSARI	151st–152nd	34th
63rd	CIRENE	157th–158th (LIGURIA Bde)	45th
48th	TARO	207th–208th	
53rd	AREZZO	225th–226th	53rd
105th	ROVIGO	227th–228th	117th
11th	BRENNERO	231st–232nd (AVELLINO Bde)	9th
152nd	PICENO	235th–236th	152nd
154th	MURGE	259th–260th	14th
156th	VICENZA	277th–278th–279th	
158th	ZARA	291st–292nd	
	AFRICA	formed by units stationed in East Africa	
21st	GRANATIERI DI SARDEGNA	1st–2nd–3rd Gren.	13th
	GRANATIERI DI SAVOIA	10th–11th–12th Gren.	3rd

Parachute Divisions

No.	Title	Parachute Regiments	Artillery Regiment
184th	NEMBO	183rd–184th–185th	184th
185th	FOLGORE	186th–187th	185th

Armoured Divisions

No.	Title	Tank Regiment	Armd Regt Artillery	Bersaglieri Regt
132nd	ARIETE	32nd	132nd	8th
133rd	LITTORIO	33rd	133rd	12th
134th	CENTAURO	31st	131st	5th
136th	GIOVANI FASCISTI	3 bns	1 regt	3 bns

'Celere' Divisions

No.	Title	Cavalry Regiments	Celere Art. Regt	Bersaglieri Regt
1st	EUGENIO DI SAVOIA	14th ALESSANDRIA 12th SALUZZO	1st	11th
2nd	EMANUELE FILIBERTO	9th Lanc. FIRENZE 10th Lanc. VITTORIO EMANUELE II	2nd	6th
3rd	PRINCIPE AMEDEO DI AOSTA	3rd Drag. SAVOIA 5th Lanc. NOVARA	3rd	3rd

Alpine Divisions

No.	Title	Alpini Regiment	Mountain Artillery Regt
1st	TAURINENSE	3rd–4th	1st
2nd	TRIDENTINA	5th–6th	2nd
3rd	JULIA	8th–9th	3rd
4th	CUNEENSE	1st–2nd	4th
5th	PUSTERIA	7th–11th	5th
6th	ALPI GRAIE	10th–12th	6th

Plate 46. Divisional Arm Shields

Divisional arm shields were adopted in the mid-1930s for the newly formed divisions. They were of identical design, but had different background colour and divisional titles.

Infantry divisions were on a blue background if in enamel, black if on a painted background. Some others were woven and some embroidered.

The badge illustrated, that of the 27th *Sila* Infantry Division, was used during the Abyssinian campaign. Later, the 27th Division was renamed *Brescia* and took part in the North African campaign. The Italian infantry divisions were not motorised. The 61st *Sirte* Infantry Division wore a red embroidered divisional badge and was one of the nine infantry divisions called *Autotrasportabile tipo Africa Settentrionale*. Theoretically, they could be mechanically transported by Army Corps, which was in charge of transport.

The 1st *Trento* Motorised Infantry Division, later numbered 102nd, together with the *Trieste* Division, were the only fully motorised infantry divisions and wore the divisional badge on red backgrounds.

Celere means fast or swift, and the three divisions so named were an amalgamation of motorised units, cavalry units, cyclist and light tank units, with divisional badges on the red motorisation background.

It is worth noting that the traditional colours seem inverted; red had always been the colour of the infantry, while blue was the colour of motorisation.

Alpine divisions wore green badges with roman or arabic numerals, and the Frontier Guard also wore green with the sector number in the centre. Represented here is a woven badge for other ranks.

Arm and Breast Badges

Guastatori were special battalions of assault engineers, trained in laying and lifting minefields, and handling explosives.

The large badge numbered '1' was worn on the breast by parachutists of the Libyan Battalion, which existed between 1938 and 1941. The breast badge numbered '4' was that of a parachute battalion formed in Libya by Italian volunteers in 1938 and disbanded in 1941. Badge No. '3' was the breast badge worn by the first units of parachutists raised in Italy and the badge No. '2' was the arm badge later adopted by all parachute units and worn until recent years.

The 'assault' arm badge was introduced during World War 1. It was in metal or worsted or wire embroidered.

Cap Badges

During World War 2 a number of cap badges were hand-embroidered in black rayon instead of gold wire. They were different from the other rank cap badges in size and appearance, as they were embroidered on a raised cardboard backing (e.g. Medical Corps) while the other ranks' cap badges were always flat. The *Alpini* badge illustrated is that worn during World War 2; another pattern was worn before then and yet another pattern was adopted in the 1950s.

Bersaglieri wore brass badges on the feathered hat. The officer's cap badge is that of the 7th Regiment, illustrated; that of the 5th is the cap badge for other ranks.

Other Badges

Other badges not yet dealt with are the two badges at the bottom left. They are: 1. gilded pioneer badge (40 × 50 mm), for gilded brass shoulder boards, as worn on grey-green full dress uniform in use from 1934; 2. silvered infantry badge worn on metal epaulettes; 3. brass shoulder plates, issued in 1934 to sergeants, corporals and privates and worn on the shoulder straps for guard, parade and special duties. The grenadiers also wore another brass plate (4) attached on each of the ammunition pouches.

The Fascist Militia

The first Fascist squads were raised in 1919 and, in the summer of 1922, they were grouped and organised as a national militia.

After the 'March on Rome' on 28 October, 1922, Benito Mussolini became Prime Minister and, as President of the Fascist Grand Council, one of his first tasks was the reorganisation of the militia which, by a Royal Decree of 1 February, 1923, became the *Milizia Volontaria Sicurezza Nazionale* (M.V.S.N.).

Originally, the M.V.S.N. was divided into fifteen 'Zones', plus an independent Group in Calabria. The Fascist 'Zone' represented the recruiting area of an M.V.S.N. division.

The Fascist Militia was organised on the pattern of the old Roman Army; its units and rank titles were basically as follows:

Unit	*Rank*
Zona—Division	*Luogotenente Generale*—Major General
Gruppo—Brigade	*Console Generale*—Brigadier
Legione—Regiment	*Console*—Colonel
Coorte—Battalion	*Seniore*—Major
Centuria—Company	*Centurione*—Captain
Manipolo—Platoon	*Capo Manipolo*—Lieutenant
Squadra—Section	*Capo Squadra*—Sergeant
	Camicia Nera—Private

The Legion was made up of three cohorts, a cohort of three centuries, and so on. The following is a complete list of the legions as they stood in 1928:

1st Zone (*Piemonte*) H.Q. Torino

1st SABAUDA—Torino
2nd ALPINA—Torino
3rd SUBALPINA—Cuneo
4th MARENGO—Alessandria
5th VALLE SCRIVIA—Tortona
11th MONFERRATO—Casale

12th MONTE BIANCO—Aosta
28th RANDACCIO—Vercelli
29th ALPINA—Pallanza
30th ODDONE—Novara
37th P. PRESTINARI—Torino
38th N. ALFIERI—Asti

2nd Zone (*Lombardia*) H.Q. Milano

6th LOMELLINA—Mortara
7th CAIROLI—Pavia
8th CACCIATORI DELLE ALPI—
　Varese
9th CACC. DI VALTELLINA—
　Sondrio

17th CREMONA—Cremona
18th COSTANTISSIMA—Crema
19th FEDELISSIMA—Casalmaggiore
20th PO—Mantova
21st VIRGILIO—Mantova
23rd MINCIO—Mantova

10th MONTEBELLO—Voghera
14th GARIBALDINA—Bergamo
15th LEONESSA—Brescia
16th ALPINA—Como

24th CARROCCIO—Milano
25th FERREA—Monza
26th A. DA GIUSSANO—Gallarate
27th FANFULLA—Lodi

3rd Zone (*Liguria*) H.Q. Genova

31st SAN GIORGIO—Genova
32nd GEN. A. CANTORE—
    Sanpierdarena

33rd GEN. A. GANDOLFO—Imperia
34th PREMUDA—Savona
35th LUNEENSE—La Spezia

4th Zone (*Venezia Tridentina*) H.Q. Verona

40th SCALIGERA—Verona
41st C. BATTISTI—Trento
42nd BERICA—Vicenza

43rd ALPINA PIAVE—Belluno
44th PASUBIO—Schio
45th ALTO ADIGE—Bolzano

5th Zone (*Veneto*) H.Q. Venezia

49th SAN MARCO—Venezia
50th TREVIGIANA—Treviso
51st POLESANA—Adria
52nd POLESANA (2nd)—Lendinara

53rd PATAVINA—Padova
54th EUGANEA—Este
55th ALPINA FRIULANA—Gemona
63rd TAGLIAMENTO—Udine

6th Zone (*Venezia Giulia*) H.Q. Trieste

58th SAN GIUSTO—Trieste
59th CARSO—Trieste
60th ISTRIA—Pola

61st CARNARO—Fiume
62nd ISONZO—Gorizia

7th Zone (*Emilia-Romagna*) H.Q. Bologna

67th VOLONTARI DEL RENO—
    Bologna
68th R. SFORZA—Imola
69th FOSSALTA—Bologna
70th APPENNINO—Bologna
71st MANFREDA—Faenza
72nd FARINI—Modena
73rd BOIARDO—Mirandola
74th TARO—Fidenza

75th XX DICEMBRE—Ferrara
76th ESTENSE—Ferrara
77th E. TOTI—Portomaggiore
79th CISPADANA—Reggio Emilia
80th FARNESE—Parma
81st A. DA BARBIANO—Ravenna
82nd B. MUSSOLINO—Forli'
83rd S. ANTONINO—Piacenza

8th Zone (*Toscana*) H.Q. Firenze

85th APUANA—Massa
86th INTREPIDA—Lucca

88th CAPPELLINI—Livorno
89th ETRUSCA—Volterra

90th PISA—Pisa   95th MARZOCCO—Firenze
92nd F. FERRUCCI—Firenze   96th PETRARCA—Arezzo
93rd GIGLIO ROSSO—Empoli   97th SENESE—Siena
94th FEDELE—Pis toia   98th MAREMMANA—Grosseto

9th Zone (*Umbria–Marche*) H.Q. Perugia

102nd CACC. DEL TEVERE—Perugia   108th STAMURA—Ancona
103rd CLITUNNO—Foligno   109th F. CORRIDONI—Macerata
104th S. TROTTI—Terni   110th PICENA—Ascoli Piceno
105th B. MOGIONI—Orvieto   111th F. MICHELINI TOCCI—Pesaro

10th Zone (*Lazio*) H.Q. Roma

112th DELL'URBE—Roma   117th DEL MARE—Civitavecchia
113th G. VEROLI—Tivoli   118th VOLSCA—Velletri
115th DEL CIMINO—Viterbo   119th N. RICCIOTTI—Frosinone
116th SABINA—Rieti

11th Zone (*Abbrusso–Molise*) H.Q. Pescara

129th ADRIATICA—Pescara   133rd M. MATESE—Campobasso
130th MONTE SIRENTE—Aquila   134th M. MAURO—Larino
131st M. MORRONE-G. PAOLINI—   135th GRAN SASSO—Teramo
    Sulmona   136th TRE MONTI—Chieti
132nd M. VELINO—Avezzano   137th M. MAJELLA—Lanciano

12th Zone (*Campania*) H.Q. Napoli

138th PARTENOPEA—Napoli   143rd C. RICCI—Benevento
139th PISACANE—Napoli   144th IRPINA—Avellino
140th AQUILIA—Salerno   145th SORRENTINA—Castellamare
141st CAPUANA—Caserta   146th ALBORNINA—S. Consilina
142nd CAIO MARIO—Cassino

13th Zone (*Puglie*) H.Q. Bari

148th TAVOGLIERE—Foggia   153rd SALENTINA (2nd)—Brindisi
150th G. CARLI—Barletta   154th D. MASTRONUZZI—Taranto
151st D. PICCA—Bari   155th MATERA—Matera
152nd SALENTINA—Lecce   156th LUCANA—Potenza

14th Zone (*Sicilia*) H.Q. Palermo

166th PELORO—Messina
167th ETNA—Catania
168th IBLA—Ragusa
169th SIRACUSAE—Siracusa
170th AGRIGENTUM—Agrigento

171st VESPRI—Palermo
172nd ENNA—Enna
173rd SALSO—Caltanisetta
174th SEGESTA—Trapani

15th Zone (*Sardegna*) H.Q. Cagliari

175th SALVATERRA—Iglesias
176th S. EFISIO—Cagliari
177th LOGUDORO—Sassari

178th GENNARGENTU—Nuoro
180th BARBAGIA—Isili
181st ARBOREA—Oristano

Independent Group (*Calabria*) H.Q. Reggio

162nd L. SETTIMO—Cosenza
163rd T. GULLI—Reggio
164th E. SCALFARO—Catanzaro

From September, 1929, the militia was reorganised into four Groups (*Raggruppamenti*) with headquarters in Milan, Bologna, Rome and Naples.

After the Abyssinian campaign, from October, 1936, yet another reorganisation took place, once again dividing the Kingdom into zones. There were fourteen Zone Headquarters, with a total of 133 legions. In addition, several independent legions were formed, such as the '18 Novembre' in Turin, and M.V.S.N. units with different duties in Rome, the island of Ponza, etc. At the same time the *Moschettieri del Duce* (Mussolini's bodyguard) was set up.

(As they were territorial units, the Territorial Militias and Anti-Aircraft and Coastal batteries, the legions in Libya and the Fascist Albanian Militia are excluded from this book.)

In the early thirties, the militia was given effective military duties, exceeding the public security purpose it had fulfilled up till then. As, obviously, not all the men were up to the standard that the newly formed Black Shirts battalions demanded, complementary legions were formed which later became territorial Black Shirts battalions.

The Black Shirts battalions served as part of the Black Shirts divisions, or in independent groups, or as assault battalions attached to the regular army divisions.

From December, 1930, the M.V.S.N. recruited new members from the Fascist Youth, by a method known as 'Fascist Conscription'.

The Fascist Youth was divided into different branches according to the age of its members. Boys and girls, on reaching the required age, on April 21st of each year, graduated to the next branch. For instance, all *Avanguardisti* on reaching the age of 15 became *Avanguardisti Moschettieri*; on attaining the age of 17 they became *Giovani Fascisti*. At 21, the *Giovane Fascista* became a member of the Fascist Party and, being in the age of conscription, if he did not join the Army on 21 April, of that year, he was recruited by the M.V.S.N. There was a similar party system for girls and young women.

In 1939, the M.V.S.N. legion was composed of two battalions of Black Shirts: one was formed of men between the ages of 21 and 36, the other was a Territorial battalion with members up to the age of 55.

The average strength of a battalion was twenty officers and 650 other ranks although, particularly in peacetime, all units were under strength due to the fact that most members followed their normal civilian occupations.

The uniforms of the Fascist Militia were similar to those worn by the Army, except that the former, from 1923, had jackets with an open collar, which was worn during World War 1 only by assault troops. The two pointed black collar patches of the assault troops (with a *fascio* instead of the national star) were also adopted (see Plate 42) together with their black fez. The *Alpini* hat, initially worn with ordinary uniform, was later discontinued.

Plate 47. Fascist Cap Badges

The *fascio* (bundle) was the emblem of the Fascist Party. It is meant to symbolise the unity of the people and demonstrate that unity is strength. The axe was added to symbolise power.

Originally, the axe protruded from the top of the bundle. The badge with the lateral axe was introduced after the formation of the M.V.S.N. and used until 1943. After the Armistice of 8 September, 1943, the Republican Fascist Party, formed in the north of Italy, readopted the old *fascio* with an axe at the top.

Generals wore a badge showing a gold-embroidered eagle clutching the *fascio* and, before the introduction of written regulations, several different patterns were worn. For instance, generals of the Medical Corps, M.V.S.N., had a roundel added to their cap badge with the red cross on a white field.

From 1925 to 1938 officers wore a star over the *fascio*, with a roundel at the bottom for the legion's number, embroidered in gold; doctors wore a different cap badge, with silver snakes and a red cross in the centre. Chaplains had a silver cross superimposed on the normal officer's badge. Chaplains of the militia did not need to be members of the Fascist Party.

Non-commissioned officers wore silver-embroidered cap badges with or without a star. Black Shirts wore brass cap badges.

In 1938 new cap badges were introduced, embroidered in gold for officers, silver and gold for doctors and chaplains, and silver for N.C.O.s. A smaller embroidered version in black rayon was issued for Black Shirts. By then the army-type forage cap was worn by all ranks of M.V.S.N., hence small, wire-embroidered badges can also be found as well as large ones.

In 1923, three legions—the 132nd, 171st and 176th—were sent to Libya for territorial duties. In the following year, instead of replacing them with three more national legions, it was decided to form two legions in Libya from local Italian volunteers and volunteers from Italy. These legions were named *Oea* and *Berenice* and were disbanded in 1934. The following year, some of their members were drafted into the 101st Legion of the 4th *3 Gennaio* Division.

These Libyan units (Colonial Militia) were entitled to wear different cap badges.

Before the Abyssinian campaign a new badge was introduced for the battalions in East Africa, made either in gold and silver embroidery, or in brass. The latter had an interchangeable battalion number and an interchangeable disc in the roundel at the bottom. Drivers were represented by a car, gunners by crossed cannons, and so on.

Plate 48. M.V.S.N. Rank Badges

In 1923 the militia wore the badges that were previously worn by the fascist squads. The rank of *Comandante Generale* was granted to Mussolini only in 1926. Those corresponding to lieutenant-colonel and 2nd lieutenant were used solely by the Colonel Militia. The rank badges were worn on the cuffs of the grey-green jackets. They were rectangular; those for generals being embroidered in gold on a background of silver lace. Some of these badges could be found embroidered on red, the red protruding to form a narrow edging all around the gold frame. Colonels wore a rectangular badge embroidered on brick red. Various types of *fascio*, with an axe at the top or at the side, and with or without a star, could be found.

Officers wore horizontal stripes of gold braid, then in use only in the Navy. Later, as we have seen, with the addition of a loop, they were also adopted by the Army. *Capo squadra* wore one stripe of silver braid; *Vice Capo squadra* wore two stripes of red braid and the *Camicia Nera Scelta* one.

Rank badges were also worn on the left side of the black fascist fez and of the *Alpini* hat. A general's rank was represented by gold stars, stitched on silver lace. The badge was worn at different angles, as illustrated.

Officers wore stripes of gold braid in the form of an inverted V; senior officers a large stripe and stars corresponding to their rank. In 1930 (see Plate 50) narrow stripes of gold braid replaced the stars. It is noteworthy that the Legion Commander always wore his rank badges on brick red backing felt.

N.C.O.s and other ranks respectively had silver and red braid.

Plate 49. M.V.S.N. Rank Badges

In 1935 the M.V.S.N. adopted new rank badges on the sleeves to be worn over the cuffs. These new badges, embroidered in gold for generals and colonels, and in gold braid for other officers, were introduced in order to conform to the newly adopted Army rank badges. Although the militia's rank badges had no oval loop they adopted a diamond-shaped loop over the stripes. New ranks were adopted for the same reason; the rank of cadet (*aspirante*), the three warrant officer ranks, and the new two sergeants and two corporals system in use in the Army.

The sleeve rank badges for generals and colonels were short-lived, as only three years later a new pattern of rank badges was introduced, with the Army's *greca* and diamond-shaped loop embroidered in gold. Obviously they were the same as the Air Force rank badges, although embroidered on grey-green instead of on Air Force blue. After a few months a new type was devised and they remained in use until September, 1943. Colonels changed rank badges in 1935 with the adoption of gold braid stripes on the usual brick red backing felt.

Warrant officers wore their stripes on the shoulder boards, together with smaller replicas of the cap badge. The other ranks adopted the diamond-shaped loop over the sleeve rank badges as early as 1931, e.g. Nos. 16, 17, 18. Later, Army-style rank badges were adopted on the upper sleeve.

Plate 50. M.V.S.N. Rank Badges

In 1935, together with sleeve badges, new rank badges were adopted for wearing on headgear, which consisted at that time of the black fez and the grey-green forage cap.

The generals' and colonels' badges were similar to those worn on the forearms. They were all abolished in 1938. A smaller rectangular replica of the sleeve badge, but without the diamond, was brought into use for headgear. Peaked caps were also adopted in 1938 for officers and warrant officers and, initially, generals wore a gold cord chin strap which was afterwards replaced by a black leather one. In conformity with the Army regulations, generals' ranks were transferred onto the band. The illustrations represent the embroidery worn on the cap band by the *Comandante Generale*.

Benito Mussolini was granted the title of First Honorary Corporal of the M.V.S.N. and later, in 1937, Hitler was made an Honorary Corporal. Badges of this honorary rank were worn on the left of the black fez and on the left upper sleeve. Mussolini's badge was initially made with corporal's red chevrons on black, with a small fascist gold eagle in the centre. In later years it was completely embroidered in gold, losing its simplicity and original meaning. As Italy was still a monarchy, on some occasions Mussolini, who was the Chief of State, wore a crowned fascist eagle.

Arm Shields

The fascist armed forces wore a number of different arm shields out of which I have selected those used by the M.V.S.N.

There are various types, in metal and enamel, painted brass, and painted aluminium, wire-embroidered, and printed on cloth.

Members of a 'Zone's' headquarters wore arm shields with roman numerals, often painted in different colours. The General Headquarters of the M.V.S.N. had one made in brass and black enamel, and each division had its own arm shield with number and divisional title.

Six Black Shirts divisions were raised for the Abyssinian campaign.

1st *23 Marzo* Division
2nd *28 Ottobre* Division
3rd *21 Aprile* Division
4th *3 Gennaio* Division
5th *1 Febbraio* Division
6th *Tevere* Division

Their arm shield was of the design illustrated for the *23 Marzo* and *Tevere*. Later, some divisions were disbanded and others were formed for the Spanish Civil War, which drained the strength of the Fascist Militia.

As a result, the outbreak of World War 2 caught the M.S.V.N. in a period of reorganisation, and only three divisions seem to have existed at that time. They were:

No.	Title	Legions	Artillery Regiment
1st	*23 Marzo*	102nd–233rd	201st
2nd	*28 Ottobre*	231st–202nd	202nd
4th	*3 Gennaio*	270th–240th	204th

An arm shield of the *3 Gennaio* made in light aluminium is illustrated at the bottom right of the plate. Attached to army divisions, M.V.S.N. legions took part in the war and others were rushed to the fronts as independent units as, for instance, the 63rd *Tagliamento* which was sent to Russia. After July, 1943, the M.V.S.N. was disbanded and its units partially absorbed by the Italian regular army.

U.S.S.R.

The Red Army of Workers and Peasants

World War 1 left Russia impoverished. Millions of men had died during the actual war and famine and epidemics followed in the strife of civil war.

The Army was reorganised on a revolutionary basis, with 23 February, 1918, becoming the official birthdate of the newly-formed Red Army of Workers and Peasants.

Officers' titles were replaced by a direct title of command; for instance, a colonel was referred to as a regimental commander and, at the lowest end of the scale, the rank of corporal became that of section commander. The same applied to generals who, by the first Red Army regulations of 1919, became commanders of brigades, divisions, etc.

The military and industrial resources of the U.S.S.R. have always been linked and the first Five Year Plan was eventually launched on 1 October, 1928, with the industrialisation of the U.S.S.R. as its main object. During the second Five Year Plan the Armed Forces in particular were greatly modernised.

The Army was mechanised and armoured units were organised, divided into tank brigades and mechanised brigades. Units specialised in chemical warfare were formed and paratroopers were already trained on a large scale in the early 1930s.

Before 1927, there were two part-time military organisations intended to promote the interest of the masses in military matters: one was the 'OSO', the Association for Collaboration in National Defence. The other was the 'AVIAKHIM' which was formed by the amalgamation of two organisations: that of the Friends of Aviation and of the Friends of Defence and Chemical Industries.

On 23 January, 1927, the OSO and AVIAKHIM merged into 'OSO-AVIAKHIM', which subsequently gave training to hundreds of thousands of young men.

In 1919 uniforms for both ordinary soldiers and commanders were alike. It is interesting to note that the first red star cap badges had a hammer and a plough in the centre; it was not until later that the well-known sickle replaced the plough as the symbol of agriculture.

There are no regimental badges in the Red Army, but great importance has always been given to the different branches of the Army. Each corps or service was represented by its colour which was then shown on the collar patches, piping and frog fasteners of the greatcoat and tunic; as a backing colour under the rank badges, and as a felt backing under the red star on the field cap.

In 1919 the colours of the services were:

Infantry	raspberry red
Cavalry	blue
Artillery	orange yellow
Engineers	black
Border Guards	pale sage green

The various engineer branches were known as a whole as Technical Troops.

In the early 1920s, new collar patches were adopted as the previous ones were insufficient or inadequate to meet the needs of the growing army. Worn by all ranks, they were:

Infantry	raspberry red with black piping
Cavalry	blue with black piping
Artillery	black with red piping
Engineers	black with blue piping
Administrative Service	dark green with red piping

Coloured piping and bands, which are considered as subsidiaries of the uniform in other armies, take the place of badges in the Red Army. For instance, a sniper would wear an infantry shirt-tunic with normal infantry collar patches, plus a vertical raspberry red stripe of material sewn along the tunic's front overlap.

Each corps or service branch of the Red Army offers an independent career which can lead to the highest rank of Supreme Marshal.

Uniforms were grey and, initially, only summer uniforms were khaki. However, from the 1920s khaki became the colour of all army uniforms, with the exception of the armoured troops who also adopted some steel-grey uniforms, symbolising the metallic colour of the tanks.

Characteristic Russian garments were the pointed field cap called *budionowka* and the shirt-tunic. Cossack troops were entitled to wear their traditional uniforms.

The *budionowka* was named after General Budienny who, during the Revolution, introduced this cap for the cavalry troops under his command.

In 1935, army dress regulations provided Russian officers with a khaki parade and a khaki field uniform. The greatcoats were grey, steel-grey for armoured troops, with two rows of four buttons for officers; the greatcoats of the other ranks did not show the buttons.

The generals' uniform was redesigned in 1940: they were provided with a new grey parade uniform and matching greatcoat, a khaki uniform and also a white summer outfit. The uniforms of the officers and other ranks remained basically the same until 1943 when new uniforms were introduced for all ranks.

The traditional Soviet badges were entirely modified; shoulder boards were adopted to show the rank, the badge and the colour of the branch of service, the latter in the form of stripes and piping. Marshals wore oak leaves and generals, laurel leaves, and cuff patches were introduced as well.

These new uniforms saw the Red Army through the latter stages of World War 2 until the final victory.

Plate 51. Cap Badges and Collar Patches

The red star, made of brass and red enamel, was the cap badge worn by all ranks of the Red Army until 1940, when a different badge was adopted by the generals.

The red star with hammer and sickle was introduced in 1922 and two types of it were initially made for the Red Army. The 'rounded' star which is still in use nowadays was actually adopted on 3 April, 1922, but another pattern with straight points ('sharp') was also adopted on 11 July of the same year. The latter star slowly went into disuse.

The red star was worn on its own on the peaked cap and fur hat, while on the field cap it was worn on a star-shaped coloured cloth backing. The cap badge was worn on the *budionowka* above a very large backing star (illustrated), but on the forage cap the backing just protruded below the metal star. The colours were: red for generals, raspberry red for the infantry, blue for the cavalry and black for the artillery, engineers, armoured troops and chemical service. Personnel of the non-combatant services wore dark green backing under the red star.

On the peaked cap, the red star was worn on the cap band, over the chinstrap. Coloured cap bands distinguished the different branches of the Red Army and in 1935 they were as follows:

Generals	red
Infantry	raspberry red
Staff College	raspberry red, white piping
Cavalry	blue, black piping
Artillery and Armour	black (velvet), red piping
Engineers	black, blue piping
Chemical Warfare	black, black piping
Services	dark green, red piping

Basically, the colours of the collar patches were the same.

Army Rank Badges (Pl. 52-54, also Pl. 56-57)

All officers' titles had disappeared during the Revolution and new rank symbols were devised for the new 'commanders' in the field. In 1919, the junior commanders' (N.C.O.s') badge was a red equilateral triangle (3 ranks), the commanders' (officers') badge was a red square (4 ranks) and that for senior commanders (generals) was a red diamond (4 ranks). These triangles, squares and diamonds were made of red felt and were worn in a line, one for each rank, below a red star on both forearms, above the cuffs.

On the 31 January, 1922, a new type of rank badge was introduced. It continued to be worn on the forearms and had an additional rank, that of chief commander, represented by a gold triangle below a red star with gold edgings.

The triangles, squares or diamonds were now set one over the other; red for field army commanders, blue for those of the Administrative Services.

By Army Order of 20 June, 1924, the red triangles, squares and diamonds, now made in metal and red enamel, were moved onto the collar patches, and by an army regulation of the following October, the order of the ranks was rearranged. The commanders were divided into four classes:

Supreme commanders (generals) with 1–4 red diamonds
Senior or superior commanders (senior officers), 1–3 red rectangles
(middle) commanders (junior officers), 1–4 red squares
Junior commanders (N.C.O.s), 1–4 red triangles

All ranks of the Red Army wore the same collar patches until the publication of the new, 1935 regulations, brought in on 3 December, which granted gold piping for all officers' collar patches, together with many other changes and improvements to the Soviet military establishment.

The Army was basically divided into three branches: the Field Army, the Political Organisation and the non-combatant Administrative Services. They all wore different badges, illustrated in the three following plates.

The collar patches remained the main feature of the uniform, showing the colour of the arm or service as well as the rank. Three types of officers' collar patch are illustrated on Plate 51: those worn on the khaki tunic, the steel-grey jacket of the armoured troops, and the greatcoat, respectively.

Plate 52. Army Rank Badges
The rank badges adopted in December, 1935, remained in use until July, 1940, when new dress regulations were approved.

The ranks should be read from left to right and from top to bottom.

In 1935 the rank of Marshal of the Soviet Union was instituted. Five generals were promoted to this rank: they were Voroshilov, the Commissar for Defence, Blyukher, the Commander of the Far-Eastern Army, the Chief of Staff, General Tukhachevsky, General Yegorov and Budienny, the Director of Cavalry.

The generals kept to their commander titles while the ordinary rank title was re-introduced for all the other officers, from colonel to lieutenant. The rank of junior lieutenant was instituted only in 1937, and that of lieutenant-colonel in 1940. The Soviet Army nowadays still retains the three lieutenants' ranks.

The 1935 regulations also prescribed the wearing of officers' rank badges on the forearms of the tunic, jacket and greatcoat, in the form of a chevron. These chevrons were 'V' shaped at an angle of 90° and were 6 cm wide at the sides.

The generals' chevrons were made of 15 mm gold braid; those for Commander of Army (1st rank) and Marshal of the Soviet Union consisted of a wider chevron (30 mm), that of the latter in gold and red (15 mm). They also wore a five-pointed gold embroidered 'sharp' star above each chevron, the same for both ranks. The star worn on the greatcoat had a diameter of 60 mm, that on the tunic and jacket 50 mm.

The chevrons of all the other officers, except colonels, were red: lieutenants wore chevrons made of 7·5 mm stripes of red braid. The other officers had 15 mm braid, while colonels also had 15 mm wide braid but with additional gold edgings.

The collar patches of tunics and jackets were 10 cm long and 32·5 mm wide, including the piping. The greatcoat collar patches were 11 cm long and 9 cm wide. Marshals wore only the latter type of patch, both on the tunics and greatcoat, with a large gold star embroidered in the centre of it. The star was similar to that worn on the cuffs.

The commanders of Army wore four red diamonds on their collar patches and the Commander of Army (1st rank) wore the diamonds and a 22 mm, gold-embroidered star, as well as a different type of chevron on the forearms.

By the new regulations, gold piping was adopted on all army officers' collar patches. The coloured piping previously worn only around the patches was then transferred to the edges of tunic and jacket collar and cuffs, and also as a piping along the seams of the officers' trousers.

Plate 53. Army Rank Badges

Political Personnel

The political personnel consisted of the commissars and *politruks* attached to all the different formations of the Army.

They wore collar patches with coloured piping as did the other ranks, with the usual enamel badges of rank pinned onto them. Political personnel was also distinguished from Army personnel by the star that both commissars and *politruks* wore on the forearms. Commissars of Army (1st rank) wore a 'sharp', gold-embroidered star the same as that worn by the corresponding army rank, but without chevron. All the other commissars and *politruks* had a red worsted star with a gold hammer and sickle in the centre instead. The star was 55 mm diameter and was sewn onto the sleeve with red silk 80 mm above the cuff on the tunic, 100 mm above the cuff on the greatcoat.

The rank of junior *politruk* was instituted in 1937. It was shown by two red enamelled squares, corresponding to the army rank of lieutenant. No rank inferior to that was ever instituted

The colours of the collar patches and pipings were as follows:

	Collar Patch	Piping
Infantry	raspberry red	black
Cavalry	blue	black
Artillery	black	red
Armoured Corps	black (velvet)	red
Engineers	black	blue
Chemical Service	black	black
Military Economic Administration, Medical and Veterinary Services	dark green	red

Plate 54. Army Rank Badges
Administrative Personnel and Junior Commanders

The same collar patch and piping colours as those above were worn by junior commanders and soldiers of the army.

Personnel of the Military Economic and Administrative Department, together with medical and veterinary personnel wore dark green collar patches with red piping. The different services were distinguished by additional metal badges, and the officers' titles also differed from those of the combatant or political personnel of the Army.

Illustrated here are the collar patches as worn on the field uniform.

Plate 55. Collar Badges

Metal collar badges were worn by all ranks on the collar patches. They were intended further to identify the branch of service of the wearer, as often the colours of the collar patch and piping were inadequate for this purpose. This was particularly so in the case of officers, who all wore gold piping on the collar patches.

The first Red Army dress regulations to mention collar badges were those of 31 January, 1922, in which about forty badges received official approval. In the following years many badges were changed and others discontinued. For this reason the badges illustrated have been divided into two sections: those worn before the publication of the 1936 regulatons and those badges adopted in 1936 and in later years. Badges from both sections were worn by various units during World War 2.

All ranks wore brass badges on the collar, with the exception of Veterinaries, who had the same badges as the Medical Department, but made of white metal instead of brass.

In 1943, when the badges were transferred onto the shoulder boards, those of officers were of silver when worn on gold shoulder boards, of gold when worn on silver shoulder boards. Other ranks' badges were made in brass.

As the distinctive raspberry red collar patch was quite adequate to identify the infantry, the badge was already discontinued in the mid-1920s. The badge of the border guards and machine-gunners still appeared in the 1924 regulations, but not in the 1936 regulations.

A special regulation of 19 August, 1924, issued a proper badge, instead of the red cross which was used previously, to the medical personnel. It was not a new badge as it had been in use some years before. Subsequently, the badge worn by the Veterinary Service was replaced by one of the same design as the Medical Service, but made in silver instead of gold.

The Chemical Service badge, together with the black collar patch, was instituted by a special regulation of 2 December, 1926, and was initially on a round metal disc. It appears on its own in the regulations of 10 March, 1936.

The armoured troops went through a substantial reorganisation in the 1930s, and finally in 1936 the 'tank badge' was instituted for the tank units of the armoured troops. Armoured artillery and other service branches wore their own badges on the black collar patches of the armoured troops.

Railways, road and river transport communications have always been extremely important in a country as vast as the Soviet Union, and special services were instituted for the running and maintenance of communication routes.

The Commissariat badge was adopted only in 1942 by a special regulation of 30 March.

Plate 56. Army Rank Badges (1940–43)

The regulations of July, 1940 considerably modified the existing badges, although no drastic changes took place as yet. The regulations of 13 July dealt with the marshals and generals who were issued with a new smart grey parade uniform and grey greatcoats, both with red pipings. They were also issued with new khaki and white uniforms, the latter for summer wear. Twin gold cords were granted to marshals and generals, to be worn on the grey, peaked cap of the parade uniform and also on the khaki and white peaked caps of the ordinary uniforms. The black leather chinstrap was still worn on the peaked cap of the field uniform.

A new cap badge was also issued in order to distinguish the highest ranks. It depicted the usual red star in brass and enamel, set on a gilded raised roundel, 30 mm in diameter.

Command appointments were replaced by the appropriate general's titles, starting from major-general, and the appointment of brigade commander thus disappeared.

Although the rank badges remained basically the same, and were still worn on the collar patches and on the forearms, they changed entirely in detail. Gold stars replaced the enamel diamonds in the collar patches of the generals and a gold star above a wreath of laurel now distinguished the rank of Marshal.

New rank badges were adopted on the sleeves as well. The Marshal of the Soviet Union now wore a large gold embroidered star above two chevrons, one above and one below a laurel wreath on a red background. The General of the Army wore a smaller gold star and all the other generals a still smaller star, above a gold chevron with red edging at the bottom. The gold chevron was the same for all generals; only the red backing distinguished the General of the Army from the others.

On the 26 July, 1940, the rank badges of the other officers were also changed. The officers were divided into field officers and subalterns (the individual officer was still addressed as 'commander'), the former distinguished by rectangular red enamel badges, the subalterns wearing square enamel badges (Plate 57).

The sleeve badges were also changed. New chevrons were devised, formed of alternate stripes of red and gold braid.

Plate 57. Army Rank Badges (1940–43)
The three ranks of lieutenant, traditional in the Russian Army, had red enamel squares as rank badges.

The collar patches were those adopted in 1935, with gold piping for all the Army, with the exception of the service branches who wore dark green collar patches with red piping. Collar patches of the latter are illustrated at the bottom right of this plate. They belong to a lieutenant of the Medical Department.

Junior Commanders
The junior commanders' ranks were dealt with by new regulations on 2 November, 1940. Sergeant and corporal's rank replaced the individual

commander's appointments, and only the sergeant's ranks were represented by red enamel triangles. Corporals wore junior commander's collar patches without any triangle.

These collar patches were made in the appropriate colours of the branch of the army to which they belonged. Both tunic and greatcoat patches carried a triangular device designed to mark the angle on which the patch was to be set.

The greatcoat collar patches were 8·5 cm wide and 11 cm in length; the upper sides measured 6·5 cm on a straight line. The piping was 2·5 mm wide and the central stripe 10 mm wide.

The tunic's patches were 10 cm long and 3·25 cm wide, with a 5 mm stripe along the centre.

Sergeant-majors wore an additional 3 mm stripe of gold braid, parallel to the piping.

Different collar patches were worn by cadets of the Kiev Tank School; they were made in black velvet and red felt, with a brass badge and the school's monogram.

The Guards badge was instituted on 28 March, 1942. It was an award given to units which had gained particular distinction on the battlefield.

It was an old Russian tradition to give 'Guards' status to meritorious units. Thus such a title was granted on 18 September, 1941 to the 100th, 127th, 153rd and 161st Rifle Divisions, which were renamed 1st, 2nd, 3rd and 4th Guards Rifle Division. The title carried several privileges, such as pay and a half for commanders, double pay for soldiers, quicker promotion, and priority in armament and supplies.

The Guards formations were always the spearhead of the Red Army. By the end of the war a 'Guards' title was conferred upon 148 infantry and 20 cavalry divisions and 6 tank armies.

When, on 5 August, 1943, the Red Army took Orel and Belgorod, STAVKA (Headquarters of the Supreme Commander of the Armed Forces) conceived the idea of saluting the liberation of each town with salvos by the Kremlin guns, preceded by the reading of an official message by every broadcasting station in the Soviet Union.

Units received honorary titles in the names of the town they liberated and therefore the 5th, 129th and 380th Rifle Divisions became the 'Orel' Divisions, the 89th and 305th the 'Belgorod' Divisions.

However, as the Soviet advance went on, it was decided to give to each formation only two official titles, and further achievements were rewarded by conferring 'Guards' status.

The gun salutes, depending upon the importance of the town captured, were of 24 salvos from 324 guns, 20 salvos from 224 guns or 12 salvos from 124 guns.

The 1943 Dress Regulations

A number of regulations, published in 1943, changed the entire structure of the Red Army, as well as drastically modifying its uniforms.

The most important change took place in January when the traditional collar patches were abolished and all rank badges were transferred onto piped shoulder boards. Other badges were introduced to replace the collar patches.

The Marshal of the Soviet Union and the generals retained the uniforms adopted in 1940, although some alterations were made to the collar and cuffs of the tunics.

In January, 1943, the commanders were provided with a khaki parade uniform consisting of a peaked cap and a single-breasted tunic with five brass buttons and straight collar. This tunic had no pocket at the front but had two false pockets at the back. They were also provided with a khaki ordinary uniform and a white summer jacket. They were both the same as those adopted by the generals in 1940.

The field uniform was substantially modified also. The patch pockets on the breast of the shirt-tunic were changed to slit pockets with the usual shaped flaps. The folded collar was replaced by a straight collar fastened by two buttons, and three other buttons fastened the tunic.

Junior commanders and privates were issued with ordinary and field uniforms; the former was also used for parade and ceremonial occasions.

The ordinary uniform consisted of peaked cap and pocketless tunic with straight collar and false pockets at the back. Both the summer and the winter field uniforms consisted of a forage cap or steel helmet, the shirt-tunic described above, breeches and high boots.

Greatcoats were worn together with a fur hat or steel helmet.

Plate 58. Marshal of the Soviet Union and Generals

By the regulations of 15 January, 1943, the marshal's grey parade uniform had gold oak leaves embroidered on the cap band, collar and cuffs. The generals had laurel leaves embroidered on the cap band and on the collar of the tunic. On each cuff they had three gold-embroidered double bars.

The marshal wore a red cap band and red piping while the generals' cap bands and piping were in the service branch colours.

	Cap Band	Piping
Infantry	red	red
Artillery	black (velvet)	red
Armoured Troops	black (velvet)	red
Technical Troops	raspberry red	raspberry red
Commissariat	raspberry red	raspberry red

	Cap Band	*Piping*
Medical–Veterinary Services	dark green	red
Legal Service	red	red

Generals of the Commissariat, Medical, Veterinary and Legal Services were distinguished by silver chinstraps. All the other generals wore the gold chinstraps adopted in 1940.

The shoulder boards were made of gold braid, 14–16 cm in length and 6·5 cm wide, with piping as listed above. The exceptions were the generals of the non-combatant services who wore altogether different shoulder boards.

The Marshal of the Soviet Union wore a large, silver-embroidered star, 50 mm in diameter, on the shoulder boards, while the stars of the generals were 22 mm in diameter. Those for generals of the services were smaller still, and embroidered in gold (Plate 60).

Marshals, generals and commanders were all issued with two great-coats; one for parade uniform, the other for ordinary wear.

All the greatcoat collar patches of both marshal and generals were piped in gold, and were khaki on the ordinary greatcoat. The collar patches of the parade greatcoat were red for a marshal; those for generals were the same colour as their cap band.

The buttons of marshal and generals depicted the emblem of the U.S.S.R., while those of all the other ranks had the five-pointed star with the hammer and sickle in its centre.

Plate 59. Senior Commanders and Commanders
Collar patches, Cuff patches and Shoulder boards

The same peaked cap was worn both with the parade and ordinary uniforms and, as previously, the coloured cap band identified the branch of service of the wearer. Coloured collar patches on the collar of the parade dress tunic served the same purpose and, at the same time, they displayed the class of rank of the wearer: senior commanders wore two bars and commanders only one on each patch.

Engineers/technical Staff wore silver embroidered bars with a single, gold-wire ornament. The rest of the Army wore gold bars with a silver ornament, thus distinguishing the technical personnel from artillery and armoured troops who also wore black collar patches.

The same regulations (15 January, 1943) also issued all officers with cuff patches which were gold-embroidered double bars. They were worn on the cuffs of the parade uniform: three for each cuff by generals, two by senior commanders and one on each cuff by commanders.

Shoulder boards on the tunic of the ordinary khaki uniform and the white summer uniform were worn to identify both the rank and branch of service of the wearer. There were two types of shoulder board: those made in gold or silver braid, and the field uniform ones made of khaki material (Plate 61). However, as they were detachable, the gold shoulder boards were worn also on the shirt-tunic for special duties.

The shoulder boards illustrated were 6 cm wide, with piping and stripes in the colours listed below:

Infantry	raspberry red
Artillery	red
Armoured Troops	red
Cavalry	blue
Engineers/Technical Staff	black
Commissariat	raspberry red
Medical, Veterinary and Legal Services	red

Officers of the Commissariat were called 'intendants' and they had silver shoulder boards with gold stars and the badge of the service made of brass and enamel. Personnel of the Medical, Veterinary and Legal Services wore shoulder boards that were altogether different (Plate 60).

Senior commanders had shoulder boards with two coloured stripes and rank stars 20 mm in diameter; commanders had only one stripe and smaller stars, 13 mm in diameter. Braid and stripes were woven in one piece, cut at the right length (14–16 cm) and sewn on coloured material that, protruding around the edges, formed the piping. Rank stars and badges were always made of silver when the braid was gold and vice-versa.

All commanders wore patches on the greatcoat collar: the colour of the patch and piping of the parade-ordinary greatcoat corresponded to the colour of the band and piping worn on the peaked cap. The collar patches of the field greatcoat were khaki with coloured piping.

The colours of commanders' cap bands and greatcoat collar patches were:

	Colour	Piping
Infantry	raspberry red	raspberry red
Artillery	black (velvet)	red
Armoured Troops	black (velvet)	red
Cavalry	blue	black
Engineers/Technical Staff	black	black
Commissariat	raspberry red	raspberry red
Medical and Veterinary Services	dark green	red
Legal Service	red	red

Junior commanders and privates wore the same collar patches on the greatcoat.

Plate 60. Medical, Veterinary and Legal Services

Officers of these services had narrow shoulder boards, 4–4·5 cm wide, made of silver braid and edged with red piping. Similar to the boards we have already seen, those for generals, senior officers and junior officers differed one from the other. Generals wore rank stars 20 mm in diameter, while the stars of the other two ranks were respectively 16 mm and 13 mm.

The three services were distinguished by the usual badges, that of the Veterinary Service in silver, the other two in gold.

Junior Commanders and Privates

In 1943 by the regulations of 15 January, the ranks of the junior commanders were also modified.

The red enamel triangles and the old collar patches were abolished and stripes on the shoulder boards were adopted instead. The shoulder boards of the ordinary uniform were made of coloured cloth edged with coloured piping. The rank stripes were of gold braid (silver for the services) with additional badges, numbers and letters to identify the unit of the wearer.

The colours of junior officers' shoulder boards and piping were as follows:

	Shoulder Board	Piping
Infantry	raspberry red	black
Artillery	black	red
Armoured Troops	black	red
Cavalry	blue	black
Engineer/Technical Troops	black	black
Veterinary and Medical Services	dark green	red

The shoulder boards of the field uniforms are illustrated in Plate 61.

Junior commanders and privates also wore coloured patches on the collar of the ordinary uniform. The former had a 6 mm wide stripe of gold or silver braid; privates wore plain cloth patches.

Gold braid was worn by all Army junior commanders except those belonging to the Engineer/Technical Staff, who wore silver braid instead.

Cadets

Cadet junior commanders and cadets were identified by a stripe of gold (or silver) braid stitched around the edges of the shoulder boards.

Plate 61. Field Uniform

The shoulder boards worn on the shirt-tunic were all khaki with red stripes and piping in the colours of the branch of service. Two red stripes distinguished the senior commanders, while commanders had only one stripe along the centre of the shoulder board. Rank stars and badges were also displayed in the usual manner.

Officers of the commissariat had shoulder boards with raspberry red stripes and piping, and officers of the Medical, Veterinary and Legal Services had narrower boards with raspberry red stripes and red piping.

The shoulder boards of junior commanders and privates were edged with coloured piping and the former also wore their rank stripes in the colour of the service branch. Their badges were made of brass.

In 1943, a brown leather belt was issued to the junior ranks and soldiers of the Red Army. It had a rectangular brass buckle with the hammer and sickle within the star in the centre. This belt was worn with all uniforms and also on the greatcoat.

Wound stripes were instituted on 14 July, 1942, and were awarded in two classes represented by gold and red braid respectively. They were sewn above the left-hand side of the right breast pocket.

Plate 62. Marshals

In 1943 a number of regulations entirely modified the structure of the top ranks of the Red Army by creating a new class of officers: the marshals. On 4 February, the rank of Marshal was introduced as well as the existing rank of Marshal of the Soviet Union. Therefore Marshals of Artillery and Armour were created and they wore the silver star, with their service branch badge above, on the shoulder boards. The same large silver star, together with the emblem of the U.S.S.R embroidered in gold and coloured silk, distinguished the rank of Marshal of the Soviet Union.

The stars were 50 mm in diameter.

The new marshals wore gold laurel leaves embroidered on the cap band, collar and cuffs, faced with black velvet and red piping.

On 27 October, 1943, the rank of Supreme Marshal was instituted above that of Marshal and all branches of the Red Army were made eligible for both.

Although the shoulder boards remained the same, made of the same gold braid adopted in the previous January, the size of the silver star was now reduced to 40 mm in diameter to make room for a silver laurel wreath which distinguished the Supreme Marshals.

Infantry and all rifle units, artillery and armour had red piping; all technical troops had raspberry red piping instead.

Plate 63. Junior Soldiers' School

On 21 September, 1943, regulations were issued regarding the uniforms and badges of the students at the Junior Soldiers' School.

They wore grey uniforms of army other ranks' pattern with black leather belt and brass belt buckle. The headdress was the peaked cap, with red band and white piping. In winter, a fur cap was worn with the greatcoat. The collar patches were red with white piping, but without the button.

The junior soldiers wore red shoulder boards with white piping on the greatcoat and all tunics and the monogram 'CBY' (meaning Suvorov's Military School). The smaller monogram referred to the town in which the school was located. They were:

Кд	Krasnorodsk
Нч	Novo-Cherkask
Сп	Stavropol
Ст	Stalingrad
Вж	Voronesko
Кс	Kursko
Хр	Harkov
Ор	Orlov
Кл	Kalinski

Special ranks were given to students of special merit and they were shown in the form of gold braid stripes on the shoulder boards.

Artillery Specialists School
The shoulder boards worn at this school were particularly narrow, 4 cm wide. They were made in the colours of the service, black with red piping, and the rank of the trainees was shown by stripes of gold braid.

Military Transport
Personnel of Railway Military Transport wore black cap bands and collars, both with green piping. The crown of their peaked cap was faced with red cloth and an additional badge, the winged wheel, was worn on it. The red star was worn as usual, on the cap band above the chinstrap. The arm badge illustrated was worn on the left sleeve above the elbow.

The United States of America

The United States, as we know them now, originate from the colonial territories of North America and, before the Revolution of 1776, the uniforms followed the contemporary British pattern. Subsequently, during the War for Independence and in later years, the new American uniforms followed the French pattern, although a great deal of individuality was displayed in the uniforms of the various state militias, which later became the National Guard.

On 19 October, 1781, Cornwallis surrendered to Washington at Yorktown and a formal peace treaty dividing North America was signed in Paris on 3 September, 1783.

Many badges, even today, show the influence of the thirteen original states by having the thirteen stars representing them included in their designs.

In 1861, at the outbreak of the Civil War, a great number of different uniforms were worn by both the Union and the Confederate forces. Some regiments, for instance, adopted uniforms similar to those of the French *Zouaves*, and several such regiments fought on either side. The most renowned among these were the Louisiana Tigers of the Confederate Army and the Fire Zouaves of the New York Volunteer Infantry. Some regiments were then known by the colour of their uniforms: for instance, the 'Richmond Blues' and the 'Grays' of New York.

However, the expansion of both armies made necessary by the war led to the simplification and uniformity of the soldiers' dress and, finally, the Union forces adopted dark blue and the Confederates grey clothing. Whenever possible, regimental distinctions were kept alive in various ways. For instance, the soldiers of the 22nd Regiment, New York State Militia, retained their traditional red in the cap band and pipings. They were also issued with red blankets which they proudly sported, rolled above the haversack.

In 1862, the first actual badges were adopted as a result of an everyday incident. General P. Kearny rebuked some officers, assuming that they belonged to his troops and, when he learned that they did not, he decided that all the officers under his command should be identified by a red patch on the front of their cap. Soon the same patch was also worn by all the other ranks of Kearny's Corps, as well as by the officers. The idea subsequently was taken on by other corps and patches of all shapes and colours, in cloth and metal, were adopted by the Union Army.

They were called Corps badges. The emblem was in the shape, not the colour, of the badge; divisions within the corps wore the same shaped badge, but of different colours.

Some of these emblems basically remained with the U.S. Corps until World War 2, for example the round shoulder patch of 1st Corps or the heart-shaped patch of 24th Corps. Some others were taken on by different units; for instance, the red diamond shoulder patch of the 5th Infantry Division, which during the Civil War used to be the patch of the 1st Division of the 5th Corps.

The different branches of the Army were identified by coloured pipings and trimmings worn on the uniform. They were light blue for the infantry, yellow for the cavalry, red for the artillery, red and white for the engineers, etc. The same colours were still worn, in the form of piping on the forage cap, during World War 2.

It was not until 1898, during the Spanish-American war, that the Regular Army adopted khaki field uniform and only during World War 1 did the field uniform (model 1916) become general issue. New webbing equipment and a steel helmet, shaped like the British helmet, was also adopted. The latter was only changed to the familiar American pattern during World War 2.

The uniforms worn by American servicemen during this war can be basically divided into service uniform, field uniform and fatigue uniform, although different clothing was also worn in different climates, and by special troops. Airborne troops, for instance, wore field uniforms differing from the rest of the Army, and they were issued with high-laced boots, while the rest of the army were still wearing gaiters. During the war, gaiters were replaced by boots with attached leather anklets, which fastened with two brass buckles.

The peaked cap and the jacket of the officers' service dress were dark brown and the trousers grey; the O.R.'s service uniform was similar but made entirely of khaki material. During the war, and in later years, a khaki blouse with open collar supplanted the jacket and was worn with the khaki forage cap by both officers and other ranks.

Officers wore a dark brown forage cap and blouse with grey trousers.

The summer uniform was sandy yellow, and consisted of a forage cap, shirt and tie, and trousers. The belt was of the same colour, with a plain rectangular buckle. The tie was tucked under the shirt's overlap between the second and third button.

The field uniform and fatigue uniform were technically the same. Shirt and trousers were olive green, with large patch pockets on both, and without any badges except those of rank.

However, in north-western Europe and Italy during the winter, the American soldiers generally wore waterproof olive green jackets over khaki shirt and trousers. Even the sight of G.I.s with helmet and all the combat webbing being worn over the greatcoat was not uncommon.

Plate 64. Cap Badges

The coat of arms of the United States of America is the badge of the U.S. Army and it is worn by all ranks, on the peaked cap.

It depicts the American eagle, with the stars and stripes set on a shield on the eagle's chest. In its right claw it holds a sprig of laurel, in the other a bundle of arrows. On a scroll, spread above the wings, is the motto 'E Pluribus Unum' and, above it, there is a round cloud with thirteen stars in the centre.

The officers' cap badge was made of brass or gilded brass, about 75 × 65 mm in size, although much smaller badges can also be found. The other ranks wore the same eagle, attached on a brass disc, 40 mm in diameter.

Officers of the Woman's Army Corps wore a different eagle, on its own, without any embellishments, and the other ranks' cap badge of the W.A.C. was also set on a round disc.

A special cap badge was worn by cadets of the West Point Academy. It depicts the Academy's coat of arms and it is also worn as a collar badge by its permanent staff.

This brass badge shows the helmet and sword of the greek goddess Pallas Athene on the United States shield. There is an eagle above the shield, clutching sprigs of oak and laurel, together with arrows. The motto in the scroll reads: 'Duty, Honour, Country—West Point, MDCCCII, USMA'.

Army warrant officers wore badges different from those of the rest of the army on the headdress and on the collar. The badge depicted an eagle standing on two arrows and a laurel wreath, the ends of which overlap the eagle's wings.

The American eagle was once again in the badge of the Transport Service officers, in this case with the shield on its chest, standing on two crossed anchors.

The cap badge of the Harbour Boat Service has the emblem of the Transportation Corps superimposed on an anchor. It is all in one piece and made in brass. As the U.S. Army went to fight overseas, specialised personnel were employed to transport and ferry the troops onto the ships.

Members of the military bands wore different badges both on the headdress and on the collar. The collar badges were similar to the badge illustrated on the left, but without the wreath.

U.S. Army personnel who qualified as deep sea salvage divers were entitled to wear special badges on the left breast pocket. The diver's badge was awarded in four classes: Master Diver, 1st and 2nd class Divers and Salvage Diver. These badges were made of silver, or white metal, and were instituted on 15 February, 1944.

Rank Badges

From 1780 the rank of American generals was denoted by a number of silver stars, at that time embroidered on the epaulettes. Initially, generals had two ranks; that of brigadier and major-general. The rank of lieutenant-general was instituted in 1799. On 3rd March of the same year the rank of General of the Armies of the United States was conferred on George Washington. However, it ceased to exist when it was excluded from the legislative act of 16 March, 1802, which determined the peacetime military establishment.

On 3 September, 1919, Congress re-established the rank and conferred it on General John J. Pershing. After his death, the rank of General of the Armies of the United States once again ceased to exist.

The rank of General of the Army was authorised and conferred on General Ulysses S. Grant on 25 July, 1866, and on General William T. Sherman on 4 March, 1869. It was again established, by Public Law 482, on 14 December, 1944, and conferred on Generals Marshall, MacArthur, Eisenhower and Arnold. General Bradley subsequently received the rank of General of the Army by Private Law on 18 September, 1950.

The badges of U.S. Army officers are unique as their rank is represented by eagles, leaves and bars instead of stars or pips.

Initially, infantry colonels wore gold eagles as their insignia of rank, while all other colonels wore silver ones. In 1851, the silver eagle was prescribed for all colonels.

The rank of major was depicted by oak leaves in gold. When, later, the rank of lieutenant-colonel was instituted in 1832, he wore the same badge as a major, but in silver instead of gold. Consequently, silver rank badges became senior to gold ones. So in 1872, the gold bars of captains and lieutenants were also changed to silver. The 2nd lieutenant had worn the rectangular frame without any badge on the shoulders of the blue uniform, but when khaki field uniform was adopted, a small bar in gold became the badge of his rank.

The rank badges of warrant officers were of brass and red or brown enamel.

Plate 65. Non-Commissioned Officers

Non-commissioned officers of the U.S. Army wore chevrons on both upper sleeves. Initially, there were only two ranks: sergeant and corporal. Subsequently, the sergeant's rank was progressively developed into five classes, which have remained more or less the same since the Civil War.

Originally, the chevrons pointed downwards, were twice as wide as those used during World War 2 and were in the colour of the branch of service, i.e. pale blue for the infantry, yellow for the cavalry, red for the artillery, etc.

During World War 2, the American non-commissioned officers were divided into Line N.C.O.s and Technicians, the latter with a small 'T' within the chevrons. Illustrated in this plate is the order of rank as it stood in 1943. In 1940 the chevrons were the same with the exception of that of first sergeant which had five stripes at that time instead of six; the company first sergeant had a diamond in the centre and the field first sergeant had no diamond.

First sergeants and master sergeants (1943–48) had equal rank. The title held, and type of chevron worn, is determined by the individual's assignment. In an infantry company or an artillery battery, for example, the senior sergeant would be a first sergeant, while in a staff position, such as operations sergeant in a Division H.Q., the senior sergeant would be a master sergeant. Both men would be receiving the same pay and holding the same rank.

The rank badges were 80 mm wide, and the chevrons were machine embroidered in light khaki silk, or woven in light yellow silk on a dark blue gaberdine material.

U.S. Army Mine Planter Service
Although technically a naval service, the mine planters belonged to the Army. They were divided into Mine Planters and Engineers and wore stripes of braid on the cuffs, with an anchor or a ship's propeller above.

The Arms and Services of the U.S. Army

Arms and Service badges (also called service branch badges) were adopted by the Army only in the 1880s. They were small, coloured badges on blue discs, as the colour of the uniform was then blue.

N.C.O.s wore these badges within or under the chevrons and the other ranks wore them over the cuff.

When khaki field uniforms were adopted during World War 1 these badges, made of bronze, were transferred onto the collar. They were the predecessors of the brass badges worn by all ranks of the U.S. Army during World War 2. The officers wore the badge itself; the other ranks wore a smaller version of the same badge, but on a brass disc. The discs were generally flat, although convex discs have also been issued, with the badge stamped out of the disc itself, or made separately and attached to the back screw.

Officers wore the collar badges in pairs on the jacket and blouse, the U.S. national insignia at the top, the service branch badges at the bottom.

Other ranks wore them in singles, the U.S. on the right and the service branch badge on the left, on the jacket, blouse and summer shirt collar.

The shirt collar of the officers' summer uniform showed the rank badge on the right and the service branch badge on the other side.

Generals wore only the U.S. national insignia and the rank stars.

Plate 66. Officers' Collar Badges

The Arms of the U.S. Army were the Infantry, Cavalry, Field Artillery, Coast Artillery, Engineers, Signal Corps, Armoured Force and Tank Destroyer Force. The other badges illustrated were those of services.

Many of the former could be found with a regimental number attached above the badge, for both officers and other ranks.

The badge of the Armoured Forces depicted a Mark VIII tank; that of the Tank Destroyer Force an M-3 anti-tank vehicle. Most officers' badges were made of brass, some partly in enamel.

General's aides wore an eagle clutching a shield with the 'stars and stripes' on it in coloured enamels. The number of stars corresponded to the rank of the general in question, from one to four stars in a straight line. In the case of an aide to a General of the Army the shield was entirely of blue enamel, with five white stars in a circle in the centre of the shield.

These badges were worn only by officers. The General Staff, Inspector General's Staff and the Judge Advocate General's Corps were also composed only of officers. Chaplains wore white metal badges.

The Adjutant General's Corps badge was worn by officers and other ranks. The officer's badge was made of blue, white and red enamel, that of the other ranks was made of brass, the shield set on a disc.

The badge of the Medical Corps was the caduceus, an adaptation of the staff of Mercury and of that of Aesculapius, the latter a device long associated with medicine. The two serpents allude to preventive and corrective medicine. Different branches of the Medical Corps were identified by letters of the alphabet superimposed on the badge. The letters were made of brass or maroon enamel, that being the Corps' colour.

The Transportation Corps dealt with all types of land and sea transport, therefore its badge was composed of a ship's steering wheel and the 'winged wheel' normally associated with railway transport.

All ranks of the Woman's Army Corps wore a badge depicting the head of Pallas Athene, the Greek goddess of war, on the collar, facing left.

Breast Badges

Both the Combat Infantryman and Expert Infantryman badges were worn on the left breast, over the pocket and the medal ribbons, and were made of silver and blue enamel. The Expert Infantryman badge was instituted on 11 November, 1943, as an award for good service; the Combat Infantryman badge was instituted on 15 November, 1943, for exemplary behaviour in combat.

The Second, Third and Fourth Award of the Combat Infantry badge are represented by additional stars situated between the ends of the oak wreath.

The Department of the Army General Staff Identification Badge was instituted on 23 August, 1933, for officers who had served at least one year on the General Staff. It was in two sizes, the Chief of Staff's badge 77 mm (3 in.) the badge of the others 51 mm (2 in.), in diameter; and was worn on the right breast pocket.

Qualified Army Parachutists wore the winged parachute on the left breast, above the pocket and the ribbons; the same badge was also worn on field uniform on the oval identity background illustrated on Plate 73. Parachute badges could also be found embroidered in white thread directly onto the oval background. Badges for Senior Parachutist (with a star above the parachute) and Master Parachutist (the star in a laurel wreath) have also appeared since the war. The Army Glider Badge was instituted on 14 March, 1944, to be worn by all airborne troops trained in glider combat. Prior to the introduction of this badge the Glider Troops wore the parachute badge with a glider superimposed in the centre.

The breast badges of the U.S. Army divers are illustrated on Pl. 64.

Plate 67. Shoulder Sleeve Insignia

Coloured patches had already been used for identification purposes during the American Civil War, but the 'shoulder patches' as we know them nowadays, were officially introduced in 1918.

In the summer of that year, members of the 81st Infantry Division embarking for France at Hoboken (New Jersey) wore the 'wild cat' badge on the left upper arm and, when eventually they got to France, other units there adopted their own distinctive patches. Initially they were worn unofficially, but permission to wear shoulder sleeve insignia was given on 19 October, 1918.

As these patches were handmade they often differed one from the other; others remained virtually unknown as the formation wearing them was subsequently disbanded or another design was introduced later.

During World War 2 some different types of patches were in use: there were those embroidered on felt, in coloured threads or in gold and silver wire, and others that were entirely embroidered in coloured silks.

The unprecedented expansion of the U.S. Army during World War 2 introduced a great number of new patches, worn by personnel of the Field Formations, and of Defense and Base Commands, Departments, Theaters of Operations, etc.

The background of many shoulder patches was khaki in order to blend the patch with the uniform; therefore, when the new olive-grey uniforms were introduced in the 1960s, some new badges had to be made which strictly cannot be considered as World War 2 badges, although they are often mistaken for them.

Army Groups

Three Army Groups were formed overseas during World War 2 and they were:

The 6th Army Group, consisting of the U.S. 7th Army and French 1st Army that landed and fought in the South of France;

The 12th Army Group, consisting only of American Armies, the 1st, 3rd, 9th and later the 15th U.S. Armies. This, together with the British 21st Army Group, operated in north-west Europe;

The 15th Army Group, which was formed by the U.S. 1st and British 8th Armies in Italy.

Armies

The design of these shoulder patches suggested the Army's number, except that of the 3rd Army, which displayed the letters 'A' and 'O', as it was the army of occupation in Germany after World War 1.

A capital 'A' on khaki background was the emblem of the 1st Army as it is the initial letter of army and first letter of the alphabet. The 5th Army was organised at Oujda, Morocco, on 5 January, 1943, and therefore a silhouette of a mosque became part of its patch, the final design being approved by Lieutenant-General Mark W. Clark on 18 February, 1943. A capital 'A' with seven steps on each of its sides was the symbol of the 7th Army, and a Roman 'X' on pentagonal background was that of the 15th Army.

The 6th, 8th and 10th Armies fought against the Japanese; the 2nd and 4th Armies remained in the United States and were never engaged in active operations.

Army Corps

Personnel employed at Corps Headquarters wore the corps shoulder patch, whose design was in most cases a pictorial allusion to its number.

However, the shoulder patch of the 12th Corps shows a windmill of the city of New Amsterdam (New York). The 18th was an airborne corps and its patch symbolises its deployment, while the shoulder patch of the 19th Corps depicts an Indian tomahawk; the '2' arrows and '1' acorn in the patch of 21st Corps stand for the Corps number. An arrowhead was the patch of the 22nd Corps and the hart of the 24th Corps was taken from the 24th Corps badge used during the Civil War.

The 1st, 10th, 11th, 14th and 24th Corps fought against the Japanese in the Pacific Ocean area.

The shoulder patch of the 2nd Corps depicts the American eagle and the British lion. It landed in North Africa and together with the 4th, 6th and 21st, took part in the Italian campaign. The 6th and 21st Corps were later transferred to France, and the former fought all the way to Germany.

The 9th and 36th Corps did not go overseas and the 22nd and 23rd, under the 15th Army, became in 1945 the U.S. Occupation Forces in Germany. All the other Corps, not already mentioned above, took part in the operations in north-western Europe.

Plate 68. Shoulder Sleeve Insignia

Infantry and Airborne Divisions

A great number of divisional shoulder patches were adopted during World War 1, but many were changed or at least simplified in the years between the wars. They were worn on the left upper sleeve, and on the right upper sleeve by personnel temporarily attached to a higher formation, the patch of which was worn on the left sleeve.

The Airborne Force was raised in 1941 at Fort Benning (Georgia), and the 501st and 502nd battalions, later to become regiments, were the first units to be formed.

One year later, in the spring of 1942, the 82nd Airborne Division was formed and it was soon followed by other divisions and independent regiments. The deployment of independent airborne regiments led to the adoption of several regimental shoulder patches as well. Among the airborne divisions, only the 82nd and 101st adopted shoulder patches similar to those they had previously worn as infantry formations.

The divisions are as follows:

1st Infantry Division nicknamed 'The Big Red One': its emblem was a large figure '1'. It fought in Tunisia, Sicily, Normandy, the Battle of the Bulge and Germany.

2nd Infantry Division, 'Indian Head': a self-explanatory large patch 10·5 × 8 cm. Normandy, Ardennes, Leipzig.

3rd Infantry Division, 'Marne': the three white bars stand for the divisional number, the blue is the colour of the infantry. Sicily, Cassino, Anzio, Colmar Pocket, Munich.

4th Infantry Division, 'Ivy': its patch is self-explanatory and at the same time it suggests the divisional number. Cherbourg, Bastogne.

5th Infantry Division, 'Red Diamond': Metz, Luxembourg, Mainz–Worms Bridgehead.

6th Infantry Division: six-pointed red star. New Guinea, Philippines.

7th Infantry Division, 'Sight-Seeing': the patch represents two crossed number '7s', one inverted. Attu, Kwajalein, Leyte, Okinawa.

8th Infantry Division, 'Pathfinder': Brittany, Düren, Cologne.

9th Infantry Division: a nine-petalled flower. North Africa, Sicily, Cotentin Peninsula, Germany.

10th Mountain Division: this was a division trained for mountain warfare. Gothic Line, Po Valley.

11th Airborne Division: the divisional number is carried by wings. Leyte, Manilla, Cavite.

13th Airborne Division: the winged unicorn. It did not go overseas.

17th Airborne Division: the eagle's claws. It was parachuted across the Rhine.

24th Infantry Division, 'Victory': a green taro leaf. New Guinea, Philippines.

25th Infantry Division, 'Tropic Lightning': a red taro leaf with a yellow lightning in its centre. Guadalcanal, New Georgia, Philippines.

26th Infantry Division, 'Yankee': the monogram 'YD' stands for Yankee Division. Battle of the Bulge, Siegfried Line.

27th Infantry Division, 'New York': the self-explanatory monogram and the constellation of Orion, in association with the name of its World War 1 commander, Major-General J. F. O'Ryan. Makin Island, Saipan, Okinawa.

28th Infantry Division, 'Keystone': the red keystone from the State seal of Pennsylvania. Paris, Hürtgen Forest, Colmar Pocket.

29th Infantry Division, 'Blue and Grey': a Korean symbol of good luck the colours stand for the blue and grey uniform of the Civil War. Normandy, Siegfried Line, Aachen.

30th Infantry Division, 'Old Hickory': an 'O' and an 'H' with a roman 'XXX' in the centre. St. Lô, Aachen, Malmedy, Stavelot, Rhine Crossing.

31st Infantry Division, 'Dixie': the two 'Ds' stand for Dixie Division. Philippines.

32nd Infantry Division, 'Red Arrow': New Guinea, Leyte.

33rd Infantry Division, 'Prairie': Northern Luzon.

34th Infantry Division, 'Red Bull': a red bull's skull on the shape of an 'olla' or Mexican flask. Tunisia, Cassino, Gothic Line, Po Valley.

35th Infantry Division, 'Santa Fé': the cross that was used to mark the Santa Fé trail. Metz, Nancy, Ardennes, Ruhr.

36th Infantry Division, 'Texas': a flint arrowhead and the letter 'T'. Salerno, Cassino, France, Germany.

37th Infantry Division, 'Buckeye': a division from Ohio. Munda, Bougainville, Lingayen Gulf, Manilla.

38th Infantry Division, 'Cyclone': Bataan.

39th Infantry Division: the triangle symbolises the three states of the Mississippi delta, Mississippi, Louisiana, Arkansas. This division did not go overseas.

40th Infantry Division, 'Sunshine': the patch depicts the sun on a blue sky. Philippines.

41st Infantry Division, 'Sunset': it depicts a Pacific Ocean sunset. Salamaua, Marshalls, Mindanao, Palawan.

42nd Infantry Division, 'Rainbow': Schweinfurt, Munich, Dachau.

43rd Infantry Division, 'Red Wing': its patch symbolises the four States of New England, with a black grape leaf. New Georgia, New Guinea, Luzon.

44th Infantry Division: two '4s' back to back, forming an arrowhead. The Saar, Ulm, Danube River.

45th Infantry Division, 'Thunderbird': a yellow thunderbird. Sicily, Salerno, Cassino, Belford Gap.

63rd Infantry Division, 'Blood and Fire': a drop-shaped patch with burning flames inside and a blood-stained bayonet. Bavaria, Danube River.

65th Infantry Division: a halberd. Saarlautern, Regensburg, Danube River.

66th Infantry Division, 'Black Panther': Lorient, St. Nazaire.

69th Infantry Division: the interlocked divisional figures. Germany.

70th Infantry Division, 'Trail Blazers': a mountain landscape with an axe in the foreground. Saarbrücken, Moselle River.

71st Infantry Division: the divisional number on a circular background. Hardt Mountains, Southern Germany.

75th Infantry Division: Ardennes, Bulge, Westphalia.

Plate 69. Shoulder Sleeve Insignia

Infantry and Airborne Divisions

76th Infantry Division: Luxembourg, Germany.

77th Infantry Division, 'Statue of Liberty': the division of New York State. Guam, Leyte, Okinawa.

78th Infantry Division, 'Lightning': Aachen, Roer River and Ruhr.

79th Infantry Division, 'Lorraine': the Cross of Lorraine commemorates World War 1 service in France. Normandy, Vosges Mountains.

80th Infantry Division, 'Blue Ridge': the hills in the badge stand for Pennsylvania, West Virginia and Virginia. Normandy, Moselle River, Relief of Bastogne.

81st Infantry Division, 'Wild Cat': Angaur, Peleliu, Ulithi.

82nd Airborne Division, 'All American': the 'airborne' tab was added to the pre-existing divisional patch. Sicily, Normandy, Nijmegen, Ardennes.

83rd Infantry Division, 'Ohio': the monogram in the centre of the patch reads 'Ohio'. Italy, Düsseldorf, Magdeburg.

84th Infantry Division, 'Railsplitters': the axe originates from the patch worn during World War 1. Ardennes, Hanover.

85th Infantry Division, 'Custer': the letters read 'Custer Division'. Rome, Po Valley.

86th Infantry Division, 'Black Hawk': Dachau, Ingolstadt, South Germany.

87th Infantry Division, 'Acorn': Ardennes, Germany, Czech Border.

88th Infantry Division, 'Blue Devil': a vertical and a horizontal '8' superimposed one upon the other. Liri Valley, Volterra, Northern Italy, Trieste.

89th Infantry Division, 'Middle West': a 'W' which inverted becomes an 'M'. Bingen, Eisenach, Central Germany.

90th Infantry Division, 'Tough Ombres': the monogram 'TO', also stands for Texas and Oklahoma. The title means 'Tough Men'. Normandy, Metz, Czechoslovakia.

91st Infantry Division, 'Wild West': a fir tree. Gothic Line, Bologna, Gorizia.

92nd Infantry Division, 'Buffalo': a traditionally Negro division, so-called because the Indians used to call the Negro soldiers 'Buffaloes'.

93rd Infantry Division: the French helmet symbolises the Division's service in France during World War 1. Bougainville.

94th Infantry Division: Brittany, Siegfried Line, Moselle River, Saar.

95th Infantry Division: an Arabic '9' and a Roman 'V' interlaced. Metz, Moselle River, Siegfried Line, Saar.

96th Infantry Division: Leyte, Okinawa.

97th Infantry Division: a trident. Central Germany, Neumarkt.

98th Infantry Division: the shield and colours of New Amsterdam, with the head of an Iroquois Indian in its centre. It did not serve overseas.

99th Infantry Division: the patch is taken from the arms of Pitt. Ardennes, Remagen Bridgehead.

100th Infantry Division: Bitche, Remagen Bridgehead, Saar.

101st Airborne Division, 'Screaming Eagle': the eagle is Old Abe, the mascot of a regiment of the Iron Brigade during the Civil War. The black shield commemorates the Iron Brigade itself. Normandy, Bastogne.

102nd Infantry Division, 'Ozark': named after the Ozark Mountains. Siegfried Line, Ruhr, München-Gladbach.

103rd Infantry Division: Stuttgart, Austria.

104th Infantry Division, 'Timber Wolf': Rhine Crossing, Cologne, Ruhr.

106th Infantry Division: a lion's head. St. Vith, Battle of the Bulge.

Americal Division (23rd Infantry Division): the stars of the Southern Cross. Guadalcanal, Bougainville, Cebu Island.

Cavalry Divisions

Of the twelve cavalry divisions whose shoulder patches are illustrated in Plates 69 and 70, only the 1st saw active service in the Philippines. The basic colour of these patches was yellow, the colour of the cavalry; those of the 1st and 2nd Division were exceptionally large (14 × 10 cm).

Plate 70. Shoulder Sleeve Insignia
Army Ground Forces

The Army Ground Forces were generally composed of all U.S.-based units deployed in training, supplying and other supporting roles.

Eventually, with the expansion of the U.S. lines of communication all over the world, some of this personnel went overseas as well.

Technically, the A.G.F. was a separate service and its members wore a round patch evenly divided into blue, white and red.

The A.G.F. Replacement and School Command trained infantry, cavalry and artillery personnel; anti-aircraft personnel were trained by Anti-Aircraft Command. The Army Service Forces provided services and supplies for all army units and also trained its own personnel.

The triangular shoulder patch of the Armored Center portrays the colours of the infantry, cavalry and artillery. Army Corps wore the same patch but with black Roman numerals. Divisions used Arabic numerals.

The Ports of Embarkation shoulder patch was worn by personnel who organised the embarkation of units for overseas duty.

The Army Specialised Training Program trained young men in colleges; those under eighteen were trained by the A.S.T.P. Reserve.

Theaters

The shoulder patch of the U.S. Army Forces Pacific Ocean Area depicts the twelve stars of the Southern Cross constellation. The Southern Cross by itself is in the patch of the U.S. Army Forces South Atlantic, above the silhouette of Ascension Island.

The shoulder patch of the European Theater of Operations symbolised U.S. striking power. Within the E.T.O. Advance Base patch a small A.S.F. badge was also displayed.

A Moorish dome was appropriately the shape of the patch of the North African Theater of Operations. Similarly, the Chinese sun, together with the American star, were in the patch of the China–Burma–Indian Theater.

The white star in a red sky above a wavy blue sea was the patch of the U.S. Forces in the Middle East.

Plate 71 Shoulder Sleeve Insignia
Headquarters

The shoulder patch of the Supreme Headquarters Allied Expeditionary Forces was worn by General Eisenhower's staff during the north-west

European campaign. As with the patches of Allied Forces H.Q. and H.Q. Southeast Asia Command, it was worn by both American and British personnel. The patch of General H.Q. South West Pacific was used only by Americans.

Base and Defense Commands

The difference between Base Commands and Defense Commands can be deduced from their title: Defense Commands were employed in the actual defence of U.S. territory, while Base Commands were deployed for the same purpose outside the U.S. territory. London Base Command was an exception as it had nothing to do with U.S. defence. Its patch portrayed Big Ben in red, white and blue, the colours of both the Stars and Stripes and of the Union Jack.

Most of these shoulder patches are self-explanatory: that of Iceland Base Command shows an iceberg, that of Greenland Base Command the sea and the ice in a succession of blue and white wavy lines. The Atlantic Base Commands came under Eastern Defense Command and had a whale in the patch. The patch of Labrador, North-East and Central Canada Command depicted an igloo superimposed on an aurora borealis.

The Eastern and Southern Defense Commands administered most of the United States. The black part of the patch of Anti-Aircraft Artillery Command, Western Defense Command, symbolised the zone it administered, which was west of the Rocky Mountains.

There were also three other Anti-Aircraft Artillery Commands: the Eastern, Central and Southern Defense.

The Caribbean Defense Command's galleon patch appropriately demonstrated the area in which it operated.

The Military District of Washington was part of Army Service Forces and performed supply and administrative duties.

Frontier Defense Sectors

Personnel of Frontier Defense Sectors wore shoulder patches with red grenades as they were manning the batteries of the Coast Artillery. The five Defense Sectors, named after the territory they defended, were: Pacific Coastal, Chesapeake Bay, New England, New York–Philadelphia and Southern Coastal Frontier.

Plate 72. Shoulder Sleeve Insignia

Service Commands

The Service Commands were part of Army Service Forces and, numbered from one to nine, they administered all the territory of the United States.

1st Service Command: administered New England.
2nd Service Command: New York and New Jersey.
3rd Service Command: the Middle Atlantic States.
4th Service Command: the Southern States.
5th Service Command: Kentucky, Ohio, Indiana and West Virginia.
6th Service Command: Michigan, Illinois and Wisconsin.
7th Service Command: the North Central States.
8th Service Command: the South Central States.
9th Service Command: administered the Far West.

The composition and design of their patches suggested the Command's number. They were all coloured blue and white.

The North-West Service Command administered the Alcan Highway and Alaskan supply route. The Persian Gulf Service Command was in charge of the Lend-Lease supplies to the U.S.S.R.

Departments

Originally the territory of Alaska was administered by the Alaskan Defense Command whose badge depicted a seal with the aurora borealis in the background. Later, Alaska became a Department and a new badge was issued: a polar bear's head with a yellow star above it.

The Antilles Department supervised the area of the Western Caribbean, originally called the Puerto Rican Department. Its shoulder patch suggests the Morro Castle in red on a yellow background, the colours of the Spanish flag. The same colours are in the patch of the Panama Canal Department and its design symbolises the Canal itself.

The shoulder patch of the Philippine Department depicted a mythical sea lion and that of the Hawaiian Department the initial 'H' on an octagonal background.

Miscellaneous U.S. Units

Combat Team 442 was a unit raised among Japanese–Americans: it fought in Italy with the 5th Army. The 1st Special Service Force was a commando-trained unit formed from U.S. and Canadian personnel.

The shoulder patch of the Merrill's Marauders was a commemorative insignia as, in actual fact, this was a mixed force and no badges were worn except those of rank.

The Rangers were the counterparts of the British commandos and, deployed in battalions, they took part in operations in Italy and France. They generally wore shoulder flashes with the word 'Ranger' and the battalion number (from 1st to 6th), but it appears that a number of different shoulder flashes were also worn.

During World War 2, special shoulder patches were issued to Chinese and French troops training with U.S. units. Members of the U.S. Military Mission to Moscow had a patch with 'America', spelled in cyrillic lettering, above the American eagle. A patch was also authorised and worn at the H.Q. of the 1st Allied Airborne Army, during the invasion of Europe.

Personnel attached to the Veterans' Administration wore a round shoulder patch with the American eagle on a dark blue background.

Plate 73. Shoulder Sleeve Insignia

Miscellaneous U.S. Units

Shoulder patches worn by American, Hawaiian and Philippine units are illustrated in this plate.

The Panama Hellgate shoulder patch was worn prior to that of the Panama Canal Department. There is also a shoulder title reading 'Panama' in yellow on red. An artillery grenade is depicted in the patch of the Hawaiian Separate Coast Artillery Brigade, and the taro leaf in that of the Hawaiian Division.

A bowie knife is shown in the patch of the Amphibious Training Force 9 which was at one time called Kiska Defense Force.

A special shoulder patch, with a Greek helmet and sword in its centre, is worn by personnel attached to the West Point Military Academy. The same motif also appears on the collar badges of the Academy staff, and on the cap badge of the cadets.

Airborne Troops

Some six different identification patches were worn on the forage cap by airbone troops. Light blue identified infantry units, while red identified artillery units in the three types of patch Glider Borne Paratroops, Glider Borne Troops and Paratroops.

The Identity Background Ovals were worn as a background to the metal wings; they also identified the branch of service of the wearer. The wings were often embroidered on the patch itself.

Sleeve Badges

U.S. servicemen also wore yellow stripes on the forearms above the cuff. They were 33 mm wide, and straight, one for each six months of service overseas. When worn on the left sleeve in the shape of 'V' chevrons, each represented six months of service overseas in the period 1917–23. When worn on the right sleeve they represented wounds.

If service stripes were worn as well (Plate 65) these yellow stripes were worn above them.

The meritorious patches were 49 mm square and were authorised for wear by personnel of units awarded a meritorious unit citation.

Germany

Germany is a relatively new European power, created only after the Franco-Prussian war of 1870. For centuries previously it was divided into a number of independent states, of which Prussia was the predominant power.

There were reasons that made the Prussians an aggressive militarist people: the vast plains of northern Europe did not provide stable geographical borders and wars were the only means of national survival.

In 1871, the King of Prussia became Emperor of Germany, with Bismarck as his Chancellor. The uniforms of the new German Army were standardised on the Prussian pattern, different badges and trimmings showing regimental and regional distinction.

The black, white and red cockade, adopted in 1897 as the emblem of the German Empire, subsequently saw the German soldier through two world wars.

The field grey service uniform was adopted in 1907 and during the years of World War I it was progressively simplified. Trench warfare soon called for the introduction of a solid steel helmet instead of the decorative *pickelhaube* of Prussian tradition.

After 1918, Germany was allowed to keep only a small army employed for internal security, and this was the base on which Hitler built his army which later overran most of Europe.

The Nazi emblems were given to the German armed forces in 1934. A year afterwards a new type of helmet was adopted, similar to, but slightly smaller than, the previous design, with the Nazi eagle depicted on the left and the national colours on the right.

All the German Army, except the armoured units, wore field grey uniforms, and although several differently appointed uniforms were worn for different duties, there were basically three officers' uniforms and only two uniforms for the other ranks.

All ranks wore the 'dress' uniform, the tunic having no pockets at the front, but false tail pockets at the back. The collar, cuffs and shoulder straps were lined with dark green material and, together with the tail pockets and the tunic's front overlap, were edged in coloured piping. Two coloured patches were stitched on each cuff.

The field service uniform was also worn by all ranks, its tunic having four patch pockets at the front and no tail pockets. The collar and shoulder straps were dark green with coloured piping; plain field grey cuffs for officers and no cuffs at all for the other ranks.

The tunic of the officers' 'undress' uniform could be described as one for field service with white metal, instead of grey buttons, and additional piping on the cuffs and along the front overlap.

A peaked cap was the common headdress of the German officer. It had twin silver cords for officers and gold cords for generals. A similar, but less elaborate cap, without chinstrap, was worn with the field service uniform. This was later replaced by a field cap, similar to that already worn by the other ranks.

The other ranks wore peaked caps with a leather chinstrap with 'dress' uniform; otherwise they wore a field cap. These were widely replaced during the war by the so-called 'mountain cap, originally issued only to mountain troops. It had a soft peak and sides that could be folded down to cover the ears in cold weather.

Khaki uniforms were issued for use in hot climates, and white tunics were also worn for special occasions. Armoured troops wore a distinctive black uniform consisting of a short double-breasted jacket and long trousers which were tucked into the boots. Initially, armoured troops wore a padded black beret that was later replaced by a black field cap. Some special units wore a field grey uniform of the same design.

During the latter years of World War 2, although many 'utility' garments were introduced, the German uniform deteriorated both in quality and in appearance: the tunic's collar lost the dark green lining and the piping. New collar patches were issued, with small coloured stripes in the centre of the double bars and, in 1945, even these were discarded altogether.

The 'arm and service' colours the Germans call *Waffenfarbe*, were initially widely shown on the uniform in the form of piping on the head-dress and tunic; as a background to the collar and cuff patches, and also as a background to officers' shoulder straps.

The colours were as follows:

white	Infantry
yellow	Cavalry, Cyclists and Reconnaissance units
lemon yellow	Signals
red	Artillery—Ordnance
dark red	Smoke Troops (chemical)
black	Engineers
cornflower blue	Medical Corps
light blue	Motor Transport
light green	Jägers and Mountain Troops
pink	Armoured Troops and Anti-Tank units
crimson	General Staff and Veterinary Corps
violet	Chaplains

orange	Recruiting officers
grey-blue	Specialist officers

Administrative officials wore dark green *Waffenfarbe* and were divided into different branches, dependent upon the duty they performed. Each branch was represented by a different coloured piping on the dark green shoulder straps, collar and cuff patches.

The colours were:

red	Commissariat
crimson	H.Q. Officials
light blue	Legal Service
light green	Pharmacists
white	Paymasters
black	Technical Services
yellow	Cavalry Depot
orange	Recruiting Service
light brown	Training Specialists

Plate 74. Officers' Cap Badges, Collar and Cuff Patches

All ranks of the German Army wore two badges on the headdress: the Nazi eagle and the black, white and red cockade of Germany.

All officers, including generals, wore a white metal eagle (1) on the crown of the peaked cap, and below, on the dark green band, was a metal cockade surrounded by a silver embroidered oak wreath (2).

Silver piping and chinstrap cords were worn by officers and gold piping and chinstrap cords by generals. During World War 2 embroidered eagles were also issued. They were larger than the metal type, embroidered in gold for generals and in silver for all other officers. Illustration No. 3 depicts the latter type of cap badge; a similar version, woven or embroidered, was also worn on the right breast over the pocket.

On field service caps only a smaller eagle and the cockade were worn, both woven or embroidered in silver.

Generals' collar patches (4) and cuff patches (8) of traditional design, were in gold on scarlet. The buttons and the eagle breast badge were also gold. Their trouser stripes, the lapels of the greatcoat collar and the background cloth of the shoulder straps were scarlet.

All officers wore the traditional 'double bars' on the tunic collar and also on the cuffs of the 'dress' uniform, the cuff patches always being on a coloured background (10). There were two types of officers' collar patches: those embroidered in silver on a coloured background (5) and those embroidered on a dark green background, with a stripe of *Waffenfarbe* in the centre of each bar (7).

Staff officers' patches were embroidered on crimson and their 'bars' were made with thicker wire, in order to distinguish them from other officers. Staff officers on permanent duty at Supreme Headquarters wore patches embroidered in gold (6 and 9).

Officers' Rank Badges

German Army officers displayed their rank on the shoulder straps: three cords (two gold and one silver) interlaced for the generals' ranks; two silver double cords interlaced for senior officers. Junior officers had the same cords but they were straight, instead of being interlaced. Generals had gold buttons and silver 'pips' and all other officers had silver buttons and gold 'pips'.

The cords were made of bright gold and silver thread, or of frosted yellow or grey thread for field uniforms in order to give a matt appearance.

The shoulder straps of bandmaster officers were entirely different: senior bandmasters had interlaced cords similar to those of senior officers, but formed by two silver cords and a central red one. The double cords for junior ranks were comprised of one silver and one red cord and were set on a different *Waffenfarbe* background.

The officers of the Reserve wore normal shoulder straps with additional grey piping.

Plate 75. Non-Commissioned Officers and Other Ranks

Non-commissioned officers and other ranks wore the same badges as the officers on the peaked cap, but with a cockade and oak wreath made in white metal. On the field caps they wore the eagle and the cockade only (1); they were normally woven, the latter being woven on a diamond shaped background. A larger, grey, woven eagle was stitched over the right pocket of the tunic.

The patches on the collar and cuffs of the 'dress' uniform were double-bars of silver braid on coloured backgrounds (2 and 5). Those of the field uniform were generally woven in matt silver or grey yarn, with or without *Waffenfarbe* stripes on dark green or field grey background (4).

Armoured units wore special black collar patches with a 'skull and crossbones' badge, and pink piping (3).

The non-commissioned officers, except ensigns and specialist warrant officers, wore a stripe of silver braid around the edge of the collar (2) and on the cuffs of the 'dress' tunic, but only on the collar of the field tunic.

Regimental sergeant-majors were entitled to wear two stripes of silver braid on all tunic sleeves.

On fatigue tunics sergeants wore their rank badges in the form of a stripe surmounted by chevrons; regimental sergeant-majors wore two stripes.

The silver braid stripe around the edges of the shoulder straps stated all N.C.O.s' ranks; the white metal 'pips' were added for warrant officers' ranks, although officially they were still known as sergeants.

Ensigns and specialist warrant officers (of the Artillery, Medical and Veterinary Corps, Pharmacists and Paymasters) were entitled to wear officers' headdress.

Warrant officers specialising in Defence and Fortification Works wore interlaced black and grey cords on the shoulder straps, with the cogwheel badge and 'pips' in white metal.

Warrant officers who were farrier instructors wore yellow interlaced cords on a crimson background with horseshoes and 'pips' in white metal.

The corporals and senior privates wore their rank badges on the left upper sleeve.

In peacetime, and during the first years of the war, the private's shoulder straps were intended to show the arm or service of the wearer in the form of coloured pipings and coloured figures and letters embroidered in the centre of the shoulder strap. The shoulder straps were then made in dark green cloth and, for instance, a red piping and red regimental number showed that the shoulder strap belonged to the artillery. Pink *Waffenfarbe* on black shoulder straps was worn by armoured units etc. Members of the *Grossdeutschland* Division had the letters 'GD', interlaced, embroidered on the shoulder straps in white, the colour of the infantry.

Plate 76. Arm Badges
Standard bearers wore a special badge on the right upper sleeve. It depicted two crossed regimental colours, with a black eagle clutching the swastika with a sprig of oak below it.

In August, 1944, snipers were granted a badge with 3 classes, 1st, 2nd and 3rd, which was to be worn on the right forearm. This was an embroidered badge: the 1st class had an oval gold cord frame, the 2nd class had silver cord and the 3rd class had no frame at all.

The Jäger (Rifle) Regiments' badge was three oak leaves with an acorn near the stem. A white metal version was worn on the headdress and an embroidered or woven one on the right upper sleeve, the latter enclosed in an oval frame.

The badge of the German mountain troops depicted an edelweiss; a white metal version was worn on the headdress and a woven oval version on the right upper sleeve. A similar badge in enamel, showing only the flower, with the the title *Heeresbergführer* below, was worn on the left breast pocket by the army's mountain guides.

Among the specialist's badges, those of helmsman and signaller were worn on the left upper sleeve, above the chevrons. Gunlayers and smoke troops operators (in other countries this section of the army was usually referred to as the Chemical Service) wore their badge on the left forearm. All the other badges worn by specialist non-commissioned officers and cadets, were sewn on the right forearm.

The badges for Army Specialists were embroidered on dark green cloth, while those for SS Specialists were on black.

The gothic letters, translated *literally*, are as follows:

F	*Feurwerker*—fireworker
G	*Geschirrmeister*—harness master
B	*Brieftaubenmeister*—pigeon-post master
Fp	*Festungspioner*—fortifications pioneer
Ts	*Truppensattlermeister*—troop saddler master
V	*Verwaltung*—administration
W	*Wallmeister*—wall or rampart master

Cuff Titles

The German Army issued cuff titles, which are also called armbands, to commemorate outstanding campaigns or battles. They were intended to be worn around the left sleeve cuff of all uniforms, including greatcoats.

Members of the *Afrika Korps* were granted two cuff titles, the first on 18 July, 1941, the second, which had the same status as a campaign award on 15 January, 1943. It was embroidered in silver thread on sandy khaki cloth.

The cuff title *Kreta*, embroidered in yellow thread on white cloth, commemorated the German invasion of Crete and was approved on 16 October, 1942.

Another cuff title was instituted on 24 October, 1944, for the defence of Metz. It was embroidered in silver wire on black cloth, silver and black being the colours of the city of Metz. It appears that this title was not issued before the end of the war.

The last cuff title was approved on 12 March, 1945, as an award to the troops surrounded by the Russians in the region of Courland in Latvia. Specimens of this title were made in Courland before the capitulation. Contrary to the others that are 35 mm wide, this cuff title is 40 mm wide. It is grey with black lettering. The emblem on the left is that of Grand Master of the Order of the Teutonic Knights, that on the right the arms of Mitau, the capital town of Courland.

Plate 77. Shoulder Straps' Badges

A number of badges were worn on the shoulder straps by all ranks in order to show, together with the *Waffenfarbe*, the service branch of the wearer or, in some cases, to specify particular units or specialities. Badges worn by generals were in silver, those of officers in gilt and those of the other ranks in *Waffenfarbe*. At times, officers and other ranks of the same unit wore different badges: for instance, the officers of the Ordnance wore crossed cannons on the shoulder straps while qualified Ordnance N.C.O.s wore a crossed rifles badge on the forearm.

As many shoulder strap badges depicted simply the initial letter or letters of the title of the service they represented, a literal translation is given below together with the corresponding *Waffenfarbe* colour.

W (Gothic and Latin)	*Wache*—Guard. The Gothic 'W' was worn by the Guards regiments in Berlin; the Latin 'W' by the Guards regiments in Vienna—Wien. White.
P	*Panzerjäger*—Anti-Tank. Pink.
A	*Aufklärung*—Reconnaissance. Yellow. However, the same 'A' is worn by personnel of the army medical school together with cornflower blue *Waffenfarbe*.
K	*Kraftradfahrer*—Motor-cyclist. Pink.
R	*Reiter*—Mounted horse or bicycle. Yellow for cyclists, red for Horse Artillery.
M	*Maschinengewehr*—Machine-gun. White.
S	*Schule*—School.
MS	Machine-gun school.
B	*Beobachtung*—Observation.
FS	*Feuerwerke Schule*—Artillery School.
WS	*Heereswaffenmeister Schule*—Ordnance School.
KS	*Kriegs Schule*—War School. There were war schools in Potsdam, Dresden, Hanover and Munich. The towns' initials 'P', 'D', 'H' and 'M' were worn below to specify the school. White.
SS	*Heeressport Schule*—Army Sports School.
US	*Unteroffizier Schule*—N.C.O.s' School with 'P' for Potsdam, 'F' for Frankenstein and 'S' for Sigmaringen. White.
UV	*Unteroffizier Vorschule*—N.C.O.s' Preparatory School.
L	*Lehrtruppe*—Trainer units. Different *Waffenfarbe* depending on the unit.
BL	(interlaced) Observation trainer units. Red.
PL	(interlaced) Anti-Tank trainer units. Pink.

Fp	*Festungspioner*—Fortifications pioneer. Black.
V	Tank research units. Pink.
Gz	*Grenze*—Frontier. White.
D	Divisional headquarters staff. White for infantry divisions, pink for armoured divisions, etc.
C	Army Corps headquarters staff. As above.
VH	*Versuchestelle*—experimental station—at Hillersleben. Red.
VK	Experimental station at Kummersdorf. Red.

Plate 78. Close Combat, Assault, Tank Battle and other badges

The Close Combat Clasp was worn on the left breast above the ribbons. It was instituted on 25 November, 1942, in three classes: gilt, silver and bronze, for, respectively 50, 30 and 15 days of unsupported close combat, or 40, 20 and 10 days in the case of wounded.

The white metal General Assault Badge, instituted on 1 June, 1940, was awarded for three assault actions on three different days. Originally only assault engineers were eligible for it. Later, on 22 June, 1940, two more types of the same badge were introduced, with the number of assaults added on a tablet at the base of the badge. The 25 and 50 Assaults Badge is altogether different from the 75 and 100 Assaults Badge. The eagle and crossed bayonet and grenade of the former are in black, and the wreath in silver, gilt replacing the silver in the latter. They were worn on the left breast pocket, by personnel not eligible for the Infantry Assault Badge or Tank Battle Badge.

These two awards, Infantry Assault and Tank Battle, were both instituted on 20 December, 1939, and worn on the left breast pocket. The former was originally in silver, but later, a bronze type was introduced for motorised infantry troops.

The Tank Battle Badge was awarded in silver to tank crews, in bronze to support troops. As in the case of the general Assault Badge, and on the same date, two other classes were instituted, the 25 and 50 Battles and the 75 and 100 Tank Battles, for tank crews; the former black and silver, the latter in gilt and silver. For other armoured vehicle's crews and personnel of Panzer-Grenadier divisions the first was in bronze, the second in bronze with a gilt wreath.

The Army Parachutists Badge was worn on the left breast pocket by all qualified parachutists of the Army from 15 June, 1937.

The Army Balloon Observer's Badge was instituted on 8 July, 1944, and had three classes, gilt, silver and bronze, and, as with the Army Anti-Aircraft Badge, it was an award. The Army A.A. Badge was granted on 18 June, 1941, and had only one class; it was made in grey metal.

Plate 79. Miscellaneous Badges

The marksmanship badges were worn on a lanyard made of twisted matt silver cords, worn from the right shoulder to the second button of the tunic. The lanyard was worn only on 'dress' uniform.

The badge was awarded in three classes, each class divided into four awards, making up twelve separate awards. The classes were shown by different badges pinned on the lanyard at the shoulder. The awards of each class were shown by small acorns or grenades attached to the other end of the lanyard, none for the first award of each class, one for the second, and so on.

The Army eagle on a silver shield was the badge of the 3rd class; the eagle, with two crossed bayonets on a shield enclosed in an oak wreath, was the badge of the other classes, the 2nd made in silver, the 1st in gilt.

Tank marksmen wore badges similar to the Tank Battle Badge on the lanyard. That of the 3rd class marksman is illustrated; those of the other two classes, in silver or in gilt, are surrounded by an oak wreath.

The badges awarded 'for the single-handed destruction' of a tank or of an aircraft, were worn on the right upper sleeve, and were awarded in two classes. The 1st class depicts a gilt tank or aircraft on a gilt band edged with black, the 2nd a black tank or aircraft on a silver cord edged with black. Four consecutive silver badges could be worn on the sleeve, but with the achievement of the fifth, the gilt badge was awarded. The badge for Tank Destruction was instituted on 9 March, 1942, the other on 12 January, 1945. It is not known if any have ever been issued.

The Anti-Partisan War Badge was issued by the SS on 30 January, 1944, but it was given to any member of the armed forces engaged against guerilla warfare. It was awarded in three classes: gilt, silver and bronze.

The Driver's Service Badge was awarded to drivers engaged in active military operations and could be worn in gilt, silver or bronze. It was instituted on 23 October, 1942, and was worn on the left forearm.

When on duty, the German military policeman wore a metal gorget on his chest, supported around the neck by means of a chain.

Mountain troops and Jägers wore their appropriate metal badges on the left side of the field cap and mountain troops wore an 'edelweiss', the flower only, on the peaked cap, between the eagle and the cockade. Chaplains wore the cross on the peaked cap in the same manner between the eagle and the cockade and some units were entitled to wear small white metal badges between the two normal cap badges to commemorate old regiments of great fame to which they belonged.

The illustrations on the bottom row represent the death's head traditional cap badge and was worn by the regimental staff of the 1st, 2nd, 4th, 5th, and 11th Squadrons of the 5th Cavalry Regiment.

The Dragoon eagle traditional cap badge was worn by the regimental staff of the 2nd and 4th Squadrons of Cavalry Regiment No. 6 and the 3rd Motor Cycle Battalion; and the death's head traditional badge was worn by the regimental staff of the 1st and 2nd Battalion H.Q. and the 1st, 4th, 13th and 14th companies of Infantry Regiment 17. It was also worn by the 2nd *Abteilung* and 4th Squadron of Cavalry Regiment 13.

Plate 80. Arm Shields

Arm shields were granted to commemorate battles and campaigns, and were worn on the left upper sleeve, one over the other or, in the case of three, one above and two below.

The first to be awarded was the Narvik Shield, on 19 August, 1940. It was in grey metal for the army and air force and in brass for the navy.

The Cholm Shield was instituted on 1 July, 1942, to commemorate the defence of the fortress of Cholm, on the Russian front, between January and May, 1942. The shield was in white metal.

The bronze Crimea Shield was issued on 25 July, 1942, to commemorate the German 1941–42 winter campaign in the Crimea.

Another shield that refers to the Russian front is the Demjansk Shield. It commemorates another surrounded German garrison, that of Demjansk, and the shield itself was issued in white metal.

The Kuban Shield, instituted on 20 September, 1943 was made in bronze and commemorates the defence of the Kuban bridgehead on the Russian Front.

The Warsaw Shield was issued to commemorate the suppression of the Warsaw rising. Permission for its issue was granted on 10 December, 1944, but it was never actually distributed to the troops.

The Lorient Shield commemorates the defence of Lorient, France. It was instituted in December, 1944, and subsequently made there with different metals available at the time.

The last shield to be issued was the Lapland Shield. The version of it illustrated is without the swastika as the shield could be a post-war reproduction made for use after the war by veterans.

Wounded Badges

These Wounded Badges were worn on the left breast pocket of the tunic, or just below the pocket, and were issued in three classes: gilt, silver and black. The first was instituted on 22 May, 1939 for Germans wounded in the Spanish Civil War. Its design was based on the World War 1 badge, with a swastika added in the centre. Only black and silver 'Spanish' badges were awarded.

The second badge was issued in September, 1939 as the World War 2 badge for wounded.

The third type illustrated relates to the 20 July, 1944 plot to assassinate Hitler. It carries the date and Hitler's signature.

The *Schutzstaffel* (*Pl. 81–88*)

The *Schutzstaffel* (Protection Squad) traced its origins back to the National-Socialist para-military forces raised in Germany during the early twenties.

The *Stosstrupp Adolf Hitler* (Shock Troop Adolf Hitler) was Hitler's first bodyguard and later similar small detachments of trusted Nazis were formed in several cities. The SS was raised on a national basis in 1925 as an élite political organisation, so much so that in 1929, when Himmler took command, the SS numbered less than 300 men. Heinrich Himmler set himself the task of reorganising and expanding this force and formed the *Stabwache* (Staff Guard), which became the first standing armed SS unit, and the *Totenkopfverbände* (Death's head unit) as a political police and for concentration camp duties.

The *Waffen* (Armed) SS should always be distinguished from the *Allgemeine* (General) SS which were employed on territorial duties.

In March, 1935 the *Stabwache* was transferred from Munich to Berlin and in September of the same year it was renamed *Leibstandarte Adolf Hitler* (Adolf Hitler's bodyguard regiment). Subsequently another three SS regiments were formed: *Germania*, stationed in Hamburg, *Deutschland*, stationed in Munich, and *Der Führer*, in Vienna. They were all part of the *Verfügungstruppen* (Reserve troops), with the exception of the *Leibstandarte Adolf Hitler*, which was independent. An SS artillery regiment was also added to the three infantry regiments of the *Verfügungstruppe* which, after the Polish campaign, became the *Verfügungs-division*.

In the meantime, several so-called *Totenkopf* regiments were formed, and in October, 1939, the *Totenkopf* Division was formed.

About the same time another division was raised from policemen and was known as the SS-*Polizei-division*.

SS members were drafted from the Hitler Youth by the following methods: a member of the Hitler Youth applied to join the SS at the age of 18 and, on the Reich's Party Day, 9 November, he became an SS-*Anwärter* (Candidate) and was given an SS identity card. Subsequently, he had to serve in the labour service and in the armed forces. When he had completed his conscription service he was then free to join the SS but, during the war, conscripts were not released from the armed forces, which left the SS with a recruiting problem.

However, after the Western offensive, Germany occupied countries whose 'Aryan' populations proved invaluable to SS expansion.

Danish and Norwegian volunteers formed the *Nordland* Regiment, and Dutchmen and Flemish Belgians formed the *Westland* Regiment. These, together with the *Germania* and the 5th SS Artillery Regiment, formed the *Wiking* Division in late 1940.

The *Verfügungsdivision*, together with a *Totenkopf* Regiment replacing the *Germania*, was renamed *Das Reich* Division.

The *Leibstandarte Adolf Hitler* became a brigade, and later a division, and another brigade, *Kampfgruppe Nord*, formed on the Finnish front from *Totenkopf* regiments, became a division in 1942.

In time the shortage of manpower compelled the authorities to recruit from 'non-Aryans' as well. The recruiting pattern was generally that of raising a legion of volunteers, which was later expanded to brigade strength, subsequently becoming a division.

A complete list of SS divisions as they were in the latter years of the war is as follows:

1st SS-Panzer-Division *Leibstandarte Adolf Hitler*
2nd SS-Panzer-Division *Das Reich*
3rd SS-Panzer-Division *Totenkopf*
4th SS-Polizei-Panzer-Grenadier-Division *Polizei-Division*
5th SS-Panzer-Division *Wiking*
6th SS-Gebirgs-Division *Nord*
7th SS-Freiwilligen-Gebirgs-Division *Prinz Eugen*
8th SS-Kavallerie-Division *Florian Geyer*
9th SS-Panzer-Division *Hohenstaufen*
10th SS-Panzer-Division *Frundsberg*
11th SS-Freiwilligen-Panzer-Grenadier-Division *Nordland*
12th SS-Panzer-Division *Hitlerjugend*
13th Waffen-Gebirgs-Division der SS *Handschar* (kroatische Nr 1)
14th Waffen-Grenadier-Division der SS (galizische Nr 1)
15th Waffen-Grenadier-Division der SS (lettische Nr 1)
16th SS-Panzer-Grenadier-Division *Reichsführer SS*
17th SS-Panzer-Grenadier-Division *Götz von Berlichingen*
18th SS-Freiwilligen-Panzer-Grenadier-Division *Horst Wessel*
19th Waffen-Grenadier-Division der SS (lettische Nr 2)
20th Waffen-Grenadier-Division der SS (estnische Nr 1)
21st Waffen-Gebirgs-Division der SS *Skanderbeg* (albanische Nr 1)
22nd SS-Freiwilligen-Kavallerie-Division *Maria Theresia*
23rd Waffen-Gebirgs-Division der SS *Kama* (kroatische Nr 2)
23rd SS-Freiwilligen-Panzer-Grenadier-Division *Nederland*
24th Waffen-Gebirgs-Division der SS *Karstjäger*
25th Waffen-Grenadier-Division der SS *Hunyadi* (ungarische Nr 1)
26th Waffen-Grenadier-Division der SS *Gömbös* (ungarische Nr 2)

27th SS-Freiwilligen-Grenadier-Division *Langemarck*
28th SS-Freiwilligen-Panzer-Grenadier-Division *Wallonie*
29th Waffen-Grenadier-Division der SS (Russian)
29th Waffen-Grenadier-Division der SS *Italien*
30th Waffen-Grenadier-Division der SS *Weissruthenien*
31st SS-Freiwilligen-Grenadier-Division *Böhmen-Mähren*
32nd SS-Freiwilligen-Grenadier-Division *30 Januar*
33rd Waffen-Kavallerie-Division der SS (Hungarian)
33rd Waffen-Grenadier-Division der SS *Charlemagne*
34th SS-Grenadier-Division *Landstorm Nederland*
35th SS-Polizei-Grenadier-Division *Polizei-Division* (2)
36th Waffen-Grenadier-Division der SS *Dirlewanger*
37th SS-Freiwilligen-Kavallerie-Division *Lützow*
38th SS-Panzer-Grenadier-Division *Nibelungen*

The various branches of the *Waffen* SS were distinguished by different colours that were worn on the uniform as piping and backing material under the shoulder cords. These colours were as follows:

	SS *Waffenfarbe*:
Infantry	white
Cavalry and Reconnaissance units	yellow
Signals	lemon yellow
Artillery	red
Rocket Artillery	dark red
Engineers	black
Medical Corps	dark blue
Mountain Troops and SS Police regiments	light green
Armoured Troops and Anti-Tank units	pink
Transport and Motor-maintenance Troops	light pink
Veterinary Corps	crimson
Military Police	orange
Replacement Service (until 1942)	orange-red
Supply units, Administrative and Technical Services	light blue
Concentration Camp units	light brown
Reserve Officers	dark green
Geologists	shell pink
Special Service N.C.O.s	dark blue/green

Plate. 81 Cap Badges

The eagle and swastika worn by the SS was different from that worn by the Army. Initially, in the 1930s, it was smaller, with pointed wings, the eagle itself being much smaller in proportion to the wreath it clutches.

White metal badges were worn on the black peaked cap, one over the other as illustrated; the traditional German skull and crossbones were also adopted by the tank units, but later the SS introduced their own pattern.

Eventually, a new SS eagle was introduced, much larger than that worn previously, with open wings. The middle feather of each wing was longer than the others.

When the front of the field cap was too short for both badges, the eagle was worn on the left side, the skull and crossbones on the front. There were several versions and sizes of this particular badge; one was in embossed metal on a button; some others were embroidered or woven in silver.

Finally, a cap badge was introduced with a smaller eagle and skull and crossbones, all woven into one badge.

All ranks of the SS wore the eagle and swastika on the upper left sleeve. That of officers was embroidered in silver thread, that of other ranks grey yarn. Eagles, embroidered in yellow and green, were worn respectively on the tropical and camouflage uniforms.

All ranks of the SS Police Division wore police badges on the headdress and on the collar, plus an eagle and swastika on the left sleeve and the SS divisional cuff title. They adopted normal SS badges only in the latter years of the war.

Collar Patches

The 1933 style collar patches were changed in 1934 and again in 1942, as illustrated in Plates 84 to 87. The collar patches were intended to show the unit and the rank of the wearer: the unit on the right patch and the rank on the left. However, all the high-ranking officers, from colonels upward, wore the oak leaves on both sides. Their collar patches were made of black velvet. Cloth was used for other officers and other ranks. Generals and officers wore a 1·5 mm edging, made of silver aluminium twisted cords around both collar patches, although some officers ranks initially wore an edging made from black and silver aluminium cords. At the beginning of the war the SS N.C.O.s adopted the army N.C.O.s' silver braid around the collar and discarded the twisted cords around the collar patches which were previously worn.

The SS runes were worn on the right collar patch by most units except for the *Totenkopf* regiments, which wore the skull and crossbones. The foreign detachments generally wore their own devices on the right collar patch (Plate 83). Before the War the *Deutschland*, *Germania* and *Der Führer* regiments wore the regimental numbers 1, 2 and 3 in the bottom right-hand corner of the patch, as well as the SS runes. The first *Totenkopf* regiments also wore regimental numbers on the collar patch, and often other badges were worn, i.e. the lightning flash, worn by signal units, the crossed pick and spade of the pioneers, or small letters, initials of SS schools, etc.

Plate 81 also shows the *Odal* rune worn on the collar patches of the 7th SS Mountain Division *Prinz Eugen*. The same rune was also worn as an arm badge by the divisional commander.

Plates 81 and 82. Cuff Titles

All ranks of most SS divisions also wore cuff titles of the division or regiment to which they belonged; they were made in silver or grey thread on a black background. A selection of these have been illustrated in Plates 81 and 82.

Plate 83. Collar patches

A number of SS divisions, mainly formed from foreign volunteers, wore special badges on the right collar patch.

Scandinavian volunteers were mainly drafted into the 5th *Wiking* and 11th *Nordland* divisions. The 6th *Nord* was ethnically a German formation called *Nord* because it was a mountain division employed on the Finnish front.

Dutch and Belgian Flemish volunteers were drafted into the 23rd *Nederland*, the 27th *Langemarck*, and in the 34th divisions, the latter being formed by two Dutch and one French regiment. The 28th *Wallonie* and the 33rd *Charlemagne* were formed mainly from French speaking volunteers. The latter originally had been raised as a Hungarian SS cavalry division. Hungary and the Balkans gave birth to the 18th, 22nd, 25th and 26th divisions, the 21st *Skanderbeg* was an Albanian division, and the 7th, 13th *Handschar* and 23rd *Kama* were formed from Yugoslavs. All ranks of the 13th and 23rd divisions were issued with a fez instead of the usual field cap: the *Handschar* had a flat-topped fez; the *Kama* a soft one.

The 15th and 19th Latvian and the 20th Estonian divisions were raised in the Baltic.

A number of SS units were formed from Russian volunteers but their badges have no historical confirmation. Some units wore German and others Russian uniforms, complete with rank and cap badges, and an additional SS arm badge was worn on the right, instead of the left, sleeve. Some units of the Russian SS wore plain black collar patches.

The only SS badge worn by the Italian SS of the 29th division was the the skull and crossbones. Their cap badge and arm badge depicted the emblem of the Italian Social Republic. The Italian SS wore Italian uniforms and initially, the volunteer *Sturmbrigade*, wore plain red collar patches which were changed to black in the summer of 1944. Officers wore the rank badges on both patches and, probably towards the end of the war, the SS runes could have been adopted.

An Indian volunteer legion was raised in 1942 among Indian prisoners of war and it is believed that a small SS unit was also raised from British prisoners of war.

Plates 84, 85, 86 and 87. Rank Badges

The commissioned and non-commissioned officers of the SS were called leaders (*Führer*—leader) and had ranks and rank titles, entirely different from those of the Army. Both wore rank badges on the collar and on the shoulder straps except for the lowest rank which was represented by a pip on the left upper sleeve.

Shoulder straps with cords were adopted in 1933 and until 1938 they were worn on the right shoulder only. They were intended to distinguish the different classes of rank, i.e. generals, senior officers, junior officers and the other ranks. The *Reichsführer SS H. Himmler* wore the general's shoulder strap with a small badge depicting three oak leaves and two acorns.

The other ranks' shoulder straps, that initially had black and white twisted cords, were changed in October, 1934, to black and silver.

In the years 1933–34 the junior officers had worn black and silver edgings on their collar patches and all the other ranks wore white edgings. This was changed in October, 1934, to silver-aluminium edgings for the junior officers to bring them into line with those already worn by all other officers, and black and silver for all other ranks.

Before the outbreak of World War 2 the *Waffen* SS adopted army shoulder straps: those of SS generals had a grey background and those of the other officers had SS *Waffenfarbe* backing.

In 1942 some rank badges were changed and one rank, that of *Oberstgruppenführer*, was added. The oak leaves on the collar patches were also changed to a new design.

The SS field uniform was the same as that of the Army with the exception that the dark green linings of the Army were black for the SS. *Waffenfarbe* was worn in the form of piping and, the first four élite SS regiments wore a regimental device embroidered on the shoulder straps in *Waffenfarbe* colours.

The *Leibstandarte Adolf Hitler* wore the letters 'LAH' interlaced; the *Deutschland* and *Germania* regiments respectively wore a Gothic 'D' and 'G'; and *Der Führer* wore the initials 'DF' interlaced.

Some other chevrons, apart from those for corporals, could also be worn as appointment stripes. The appointment of SS-*Stabsscharführer*, given to senior N.C.O.s, was a striped braid chevron stitched onto the lower right sleeve.

The *Altekampfer* chevron was worn on the right upper arm by 'old campaigners' who were party members before 1933. The same chevron, with a round 'pip', was worn by ex-policemen who were members of the SS.

SS men who were ex-members of the *Stahlhelm* organisation wore a distinguishing black chevron on the left forearm.

Plate 88. Rank Badges for Camouflage Uniforms

There were several types of camouflage overalls for use in different seasons or on different terrain. A new type of rank badge was devised for these garments in 1943.

These rank badges were worn on the upper left sleeve only, and consisted of a combination of bars and oak leaves on a black rectangular or square background. The bars and oak leaves were yellow for generals and green for all the other ranks. Corporals wore the usual triangular chevrons also on camouflage clothing.

Index

This is not a complete Index but is intended only as a cross reference between illustration and description